CONVERSING

with GOD *in*

SCRIPTURE

A CONTEMPORARY APPROACH

TO *LECTIO DIVINA*

D1044519

CONVERSING
with GOD *in*
SCRIPTURE

A CONTEMPORARY APPROACH

TO *LECTIO DIVINA*

STEPHEN J. BINZ

the WORD among us® press

Library of Congress Cataloging-in-Publication Data
Binz, Stephen J., 1955-
Conversing with God in Scripture : a contemporary approach to lectio
divina / Stephen J. Binz.
    p. cm.
Includes bibliographical references.
ISBN 978-1-59325-126-0 (alk. paper)
1. Bible--Devotional use. 2. Spiritual life--Catholic Church. I. Title.
BS617.8.B56 2008
248.3--dc22
                                        2007047625

Dedicated to
Carlo M. Martini, SJ,
former professor and rector of the Pontifical Biblical Institute
and retired cardinal archbishop of Milan,
whose inspiration taught me the unity of
biblical scholarship and prayerful reading.

Contents

Preface   9

1. Return to *Lectio Divina:* A New Moment for the Church   *11*
   Resurging Interest in the Bible
   The Highest Goal of Bible Reading
   The Ancient Tradition of *Lectio Divina*
   Sacred Reading for All God's People
   Essential Characteristics of *Lectio Divina*
   Necessary Dispositions for *Lectio Divina*
   Questions for Reflection or Discussion

2. A Living Book, Centered in Christ   *25*
   The Indwelling of the Holy Spirit
   Images of the Sacred Page
   The One Book That Is Christ
   The Word, Abbreviated and Concentrated
   The Great Sacrament of Scripture
   The Life-changing Power of God's Word
   Questions for Reflection or Discussion

3. *Lectio:* Reading the Text with a Listening Ear   *43*
   A Ladder or a Circle?
   Listening with the Ear of Our Hearts
   What Does This Text Say?
   The Past and Present Meanings of Biblical Texts
   A Divine and Human Word
   Lectio in the Life of Mary
   Questions for Reflection or Discussion

4. *Meditatio:* Reflecting on the Meaning and Message 59
   of the Text
   Preparing for Meditation
   Letting the Word Resound within Us
   Ruminating on the Text
   Questions for Reflection
   The Diverse Senses of Scripture
   Meditating with the Imagination
   Meditatio in the Life of Mary
   Questions for Reflection or Discussion

5. *Oratio:* Praying in Response to God's Word 71
   Moving from *Lectio* and *Meditatio* to Prayer from the Heart
   Lectio Divina Teaches Us How to Pray
   The Gift of God's Spirit Released in Our Hearts
   The Treasury of Prayer in the Bible
   The Prayer That Jesus Taught Us
   Oratio in the Life of Mary
   Questions for Reflection or Discussion

6. *Contemplatio:* Quietly Resting in God 85
   Moving from Active Prayer to Contemplative Prayer
   Resistance to *Contemplatio* Today
   Nurturing the Interior Life of Contemplation
   The Practice of *Contemplatio*
   Touching the Life of the Trinity
   Contemplatio in the Life of Mary
   Questions for Reflection or Discussion

7. *Operatio:* Faithful Witness in Daily Life   95
   The Unity of *Contemplatio* and *Operatio*
   The Fruitfulness of God's Word
   Formed as Disciples through the Word
   The Word Leads to Discernment and Decision Making
   Actualization of the Ancient Text
   Operatio in the Life of Mary
   Questions for Reflection or Discussion

8. *Collatio:* Forming Community Through Scripture   109
   Forming Communities of Faith, Centered on the Word
   Practical Advice and Warnings
   Methods of *Collatio*
   Questions for Reflection or Discussion

9. The Practice of *Lectio Divina*   117
   Suggestions for a Personal Method
   Writing and Journaling with *Lectio Divina*
   The Encounter of Moses at the Burning Bush (Exodus 3:1-15)
   Elijah Meets God on the Mountain (1 Kings 19:4-13)
   "How Long, O LORD?"—A Lament (Psalm 13)
   Surrendering to God's All-searching Presence (Psalm 139)
   Jesus and the Little Children (Mark 10:13-16)
   The Parable of the Workers in the Vineyard (Matthew 20:1-16)
   The Storm on the Sea (Mark 4:35-41)
   Continuing to Pray with Scripture
   Questions for Reflection or Discussion

Notes   147

Preface

Wherever I teach about the Bible, I find people asking about ways to make the biblical texts personal and prayerful. What they are really asking is how to experience the inspired word as God intended it for us. As the word of its divine author, the Bible is not just a literary anthology of ancient texts; it is inspired literature addressed to the hearts of God's people.

My response to these questions is not to refer to modern, creative methods for making the Bible more relevant to life today. Rather, my answer always refers to the most ancient method of the church for reading the Bible—*lectio divina*. Unfortunately, there is never sufficient time in response to questions to do justice to this time-honored tradition. That's why I have written this book—to offer a concise and lucid overview of this practice of prayerful reading of Scripture.

I am grateful to the fellowship of scholars and authors who have written and taught about lectio divina in recent decades, especially those mentioned throughout this book. They have taught me much, and my work is indebted to them. I have long admired the work of The Word Among Us, under the direction of its president, Jeff Smith. I thank the editorial staff of The Word Among Us Press, especially Patricia Mitchell and Bert Ghezzi, and its director, Don Cooper, for the invitation and encouragement to write this book. And I also thank Bob French, my copy editor, who made this a better book.

Due to the increasing popularity and importance of lectio divina in the church today, I have written a book that can be used by the beginner as well as the seasoned practitioner. Suspecting that many churches and communities will want to use this work for book studies and group learning, I have included questions for reflection and discussion at the end of each chapter.

As one who has worked in the biblical apostolate of the church for many years through teaching and writing, I can testify that the combination of Bible study and lectio divina is a providential union for the church in our time. The biblical fervor among the people of God today is being kindled through the church's ancient art of reflectively and prayerfully reading sacred Scripture. May this book be for you the invitation to a lifelong adventure in Christ.

Stephen J. Binz

Return to *Lectio Divina:*
A New Moment for the Church

The term *lectio divina* is used frequently to refer to various methods of prayerfully reading the Bible. *Lectio divina* is a Latin expression that is best translated, though incompletely, as "sacred reading." It has a rich and varied history within the Christian tradition and is becoming increasingly popular in our day while revitalizing the lives of many throughout the church.

As a way of praying, lectio divina honors that most basic source of all real prayer—an interior desire for God. Lectio divina lets us understand that our desire for God is the result of God's initiative, the stirring of God's grace within us, drawing us and inviting us to a deeper intimacy with him.

Unfortunately, most people think of prayer as an encounter with God that they are expected to begin. As if starting a conversation, they approach God with their needs, then wait for him to reply. When using this approach to prayer, they don't understand why God is so reluctant to respond to their prayerful initiatives. They become disillusioned and frustrated with the whole idea of prayer as talking to God and waiting for an answer.

By beginning with the revealed word of God, lectio divina continues the conversation that God has begun. We first pay attention to his approach to us and focus on our receptivity. Scripture becomes a means for God to feed, heal, and love us. We open ourselves to God's presence and respond with our hearts.

Resurging Interest in the Bible

The renewed attraction to lectio divina today is a rich fruit of the increasing interest in the Bible among the people of God worldwide. Though the Bible has always been at the heart of Christian faith and practice, there was a time between the Reformation and the Second Vatican Council in which a deep fear of the influence of personal opinion on Scripture interpretation effectively removed the Bible from the hands of most Catholics.

During this period, the rich biblical theology and spirituality that characterized the church's early centuries remained dormant. Though church doctrine, liturgy, and practice, as well as liturgical art and architecture, taught people the images and ideas of the Bible, a family Bible in a Catholic home was only an item of pious décor before the revolutionary changes brought about by the council.

In words that are now enshrined in the *Catechism of the Catholic Church* (133), the Second Vatican Council urged "all the Christian faithful" to make Bible reading a regular part of their lives. It also quoted the famous words of St. Jerome (fourth century) that not knowing Scripture means not knowing Christ[1]:

> The sacred synod forcefully and specifically exhorts all the Christian faithful . . . to learn "the surpassing knowledge of Jesus Christ" by frequent reading of the divine Scriptures. "Ignorance of the Scriptures is ignorance of Christ." (*Dogmatic Constitution on Divine Revelation*, 25)

The council also urged the church to make every means available for God's people to read, study, and pray the Scriptures. It insisted that "access to sacred Scripture ought to be open wide to the Christian faithful" (*Dogmatic Constitution on Divine Revelation*, 22). This has resulted in more Bible-rich preaching and catechesis, as well as a surge of Bible studies, conferences, workshops, and publications throughout the world.

The Highest Goal of Bible Reading

There are many reasons for reading and studying the Bible. They range from religious curiosity, to academic interest, to a desire to evangelize others or to respond to fundamentalist attacks.

Many Christians read the Bible with an intellectual mind-set. They want to gain a comprehensive overview of the history of our salvation, as well as a taste for all the great literature that fills the many pages of Scripture. Those with a scholarly bent study the Bible in order to understand the ideas and themes raised by the text. Others are more interested in the theological issues woven throughout Scripture. They want to be able to teach, discuss, and debate the great truths of faith that are enshrined within its sacred pages.

There is one reason for reading the Bible, however, that is supreme: we read Scripture in order to encounter God there. We know in faith that the Bible is inspired by God's Spirit and communicates the word of God to us. Through the sacred pages of Scripture, we can experience the living word of God speaking to us and sharing divine life with us. Reading the Bible invites us to experience God's own self-manifestation and to respond to God with personal faith.

This highest goal of Bible reading is also the purpose of *lectio divina*. It is a traditional way of reading Scripture that allows the word of God to penetrate our hearts and leads us to grow in an intimate relationship with him. In lectio divina we trust that the sacred text will not only *inform* us but *transform* us, as well.

The Ancient Tradition of *Lectio Divina*

In Christianity's earliest centuries, it was understood that a daily reading of Scripture nourished the Christian life. The church inherited this belief from the Jewish tradition at the roots of Christianity. Jewish teachers who lived before the Christian era instructed their disciples to immerse themselves in prayerful reading of the sacred scrolls. They taught that the Torah is God's presence, to which we open ourselves through reading, meditation, and prayer.

In the Jewish synagogue, the ark containing the sacred texts is the focal point for worship. With lamps burning around it, this sacred space proclaims the holy presence. Truly this is where God encounters his people and speaks with them. Christians share with our elder brothers and sisters in Judaism the tremendous privilege of being sons and daughters of the holy book.

As a Jewish teacher, Jesus was absorbed in sacred reading of the Hebrew Scriptures. We see in his reading of the scroll in the synagogue at Nazareth that he had prayerfully reflected often on that text of the prophet Isaiah (Luke 4:16-30). From the time of his ministry in Galilee until his passion in Jerusalem, Jesus' contemplative reading of the ancient Scriptures matured his self-understanding. This method of prayerful meditation is the type of sacred reading he taught his disciples.

This ancient art of lectio divina was encouraged in the patristic theology of the early Christian centuries. Origen (third century) expressed the principles of lectio divina, affirming that in order to read the Bible profitably it is necessary to do so with attention, constancy, and prayer. The term itself is found extensively in the writings of fourth- and fifth-century patristic authors, such as St. Jerome (fourth century): "The soul is fed each day with *lectio divina.*"[2]

The desert fathers and mothers of the early centuries and the monastic movement nurtured lectio divina. St. Benedict (sixth century) incorporated it into his monastic rule, setting aside considerable time for lectio divina in the daily schedule, so that the triple base of monastic life consisted of liturgy, manual labor, and sacred reading. Louis Bouyer, OC, describes the qualities of lectio divina as practiced by the monks:

> It is personal reading of the Word of God during which we try to assimilate its substance; a reading in faith, in a spirit of prayer, believing in the real presence of God who speaks to us in the sacred text, while the monk himself strives to be present in a spirit of obedience and total surrender to the divine promises and demands.[3]

Unfortunately, this unified and personal way of prayerful reading declined in later centuries under the influence of Scholasticism (twelfth century on). This analytical and intellectual approach to Scripture became increasingly suspicious of personal experience and the contemplative dimensions of prayer. Finally, lectio divina went into virtual oblivion after the Reformation (sixteenth century) because of the strong Catholic reaction to Protestant emphasis on the personal interpretation of Scripture. With the need to control a threat that seemed out of hand, the church's prayer moved into the head and left the heart behind.

Sacred Reading for All God's People

The dominant attitude toward the Scriptures that had prevailed for several centuries within the church, from the Reformation to the Second Vatican Council, assumed that the purpose of the text was to communicate a doctrinal or moral message. When we had received the message, the text had achieved its purpose. With this attitude there was really no purpose in reading Scripture for its own sake, but only as a means to extract some specific teaching of the church.

Lectio divina helps us return to the more ancient understanding of the sacredness of the inspired text. The Bible is not like a textbook, providing objective information. Rather, it is a means of joining us to the story of God's people. It appeals to our imagination and feelings. We get caught up in the literature and experience it as God personally addressing us. In practicing lectio divina, we love the text itself; we read it reflectively, linger over it, and let it reach the depths of our hearts.

Sacred reading is again becoming a source of deep spiritual growth for all of God's people. We are returning to the tradition taught to us by the Jewish rabbis and by the example of Jesus himself. We are reaping the wisdom of the desert and the understanding cultivated for centuries through the monastic tradition. Once again, the whole people of God are recognizing the spiritual power achieved through experiencing God's presence in the inspired Scriptures. Reverential reading and listening to God's voice in the sacred text can offer a vital experience of God's living word.

Pope Benedict XVI has encouraged the faithful to restore the practice of lectio divina. At a conference entitled "Sacred Scripture in the Life of the Church," he said,

> I would like in particular to recall and recommend the ancient tradition of *lectio divina*: the diligent reading of sacred Scripture accompanied by prayer brings about that intimate dialogue in which the person reading hears God who is speaking, and in praying, responds to him with trusting openness of heart. If the practice of *lectio divina* is effectively promoted, I am convinced that it will bring to the church a new spiritual springtime.[4]

Clearly, Benedict sees great value in working to revive this ancient practice. Lectio divina is not just encouraged for certain people in the church—clerics or religious—but for all the people of God. If we return to the earlier understanding that the Christian life is one that is regularly nourished by sacred Scripture, a new spiritual renewal will emerge to bring forth abundant fruit for the church.

Lectio divina today cannot simply duplicate the practice of the early centuries. Most of God's people no longer live in the desert or monastic communities. The prescriptions enshrined in patristic texts and communal rules can offer us guidance, but not rigid formulas, for reviving the practice of sacred reading. Factors such as the following require us to modify our approach to lectio divina: today we must take into account the awareness that people are seeking solitude in the midst of secular life; that couples want to create Christian families nourished by Scripture; that we must authenticate our understanding of biblical literature by examining the valuable scholarship of recent decades; and that believers want to experience a community of faith in the context of their lived experiences.

In light of contemporary challenges to the spiritual life, Benedict has urged pastors, scholars, and writers to ponder new methods for adapting lectio divina to the present age. In his conference address, the pope stated, "The ancient tradition of *lectio divina* should be encouraged through the use of new methods, attentively pondered, adapted to the time."[5]

Because lectio divina should be promoted for all people, a variety of approaches can be imagined that remain faithful to the ancient tradition. In order to bring the richness of sacred reading to the people of God, we will need to be wise, like the master of the household in the gospel "who brings out of his treasure what is new and what is old" (Matthew 13:52).

Essential Characteristics of *Lectio Divina*

Because lectio divina must use new methods, adapted to the times, in order to become a vital spiritual devotion for the modern church, it is essential to understand what makes for its authentic practice. With this understanding, we will be able to discern sacred reading that is in line with the ancient tradition as well as practices that deviate from the vital wisdom we have inherited from the past. The following qualities are the essential characteristics that make the common practice of Bible reading an authentic experience of lectio divina:

- *Lectio divina establishes a dialogue between the reader of Scripture and God.* The prayerful reader experiences the reading and reflection on the text as a listening to God. Having listened carefully to God, the reader then responds to him in prayer. St. Jerome (fourth century) explains: "He listens to God when he reads sacred Scripture; he speaks with him when he prays to the Lord."[6] This gentle oscillation between listening to God and responding in prayer is an essential aspect of lectio divina.

- *Lectio divina is a personal encounter with God through Scripture.* The biblical text is not a book of information. Its purpose is not to communicate a doctrinal or moral message. Rather, the text itself is a gateway to God. Through the inspired Scripture, we meet the God who loves us and desires our response. This encounter with God is a communion that has many of the same personal characteristics as the communion of the Eucharist. The living word is a divine presence; God dwells within the inspired word.

- *Lectio divina aims at heart-to-heart intimacy with God.* In the Bible, the heart is a person's innermost core, the place from which one's deepest longings, motivations, decisions, memories, and desires arise. In lectio divina, the prayerful reader attempts to respond to God's word with the whole heart. St. Gregory the Great urged the reader of Scripture, "Learn to know the heart of God in the words of God" (sixth century).[7] Through lectio divina we can come to a relationship with God at the deepest level of intimacy.

- *Lectio divina leads to contemplation and action.* There is a moment in all true love that leads to a level of communication too deep for words. Prayerful reading inevitably leads to that deepest form of communication with God, which is loving silence. In addition, all true love must be expressed in action. Eventually words become inadequate, and love must be demonstrated in deeds arising from a changed heart. Lectio divina is recognized as genuine through its fruit; it produces contemplatives in action.

Necessary Dispositions for Lectio Divina

The encounter of the two disciples with the risen Lord on the road to Emmaus is an experience of lectio divina. As they were walking on their way from Jerusalem, the disciples were in a mood of dismay and discouragement—not good dispositions for lectio divina. But at Christ's initiative, they found a way to open up their lives to listen to him and to experience his risen presence with them. In reflecting on their encounter, "They said to each other, 'Were not our hearts burning within us while he was talking to us on the road, while he was opening the scriptures to us?'" (Luke 24:32).

The word of God and its power to transform us are gifts from God that we must accept into our lives. In order to receive the gift of deep intimacy with Christ, we must create the necessary conditions within us so that we can more readily listen and receive. Here are some of the necessary dispositions for lectio divina to do its work of conversion within us:

- *Openheartedness.* We can accept the word of God when we open our hearts to the gifts it offers us. There is much within Scripture that may confuse, frustrate, and even shock us and might even cause us to reject its message. On the other hand, we also have a tendency within us to say, "I know this already; I've heard this before." The only way to receive the word of God through the text is to approach it with an open mind and heart. If we do so, God gradually opens the doors of our hearts and creates within us the freedom to be completely dedicated to his love. On our part, this means ridding ourselves of as many external attractions and internal passions as possible. This purgation creates purity of heart and that full receptivity that enables us to be progressively changed by God's word.

- *Reverence.* In prayerfully reading Scripture, we are entering the mystery of God. This sense of awe before God leads us toward silence and opens us to listen. Lectio divina places us in the position of a disciple being instructed by the Lord. The teacher is the one who speaks, while the disciple remains silent to listen. God's word is always more than we can comprehend, and we should never approach it with less than veneration and respect. Reverence before the mystery of God's word instills humility within us. St. Augustine describes his initial arrogance before God: "Proud as I was, I dared to seek that which only the humble can find."[8] We must accept our profound ignorance with regard to God. Filled with hunger and thirst, yearning and need, we know that we can only listen and receive. When we reverently open the sacred text, we open our hearts to be formed by God.

- *Faithfulness.* The regular practice of lectio divina gradually creates a "biblical" person, whose mind and heart are saturated with the words, images, and memories of Scripture. But this process takes time, dedication, and persistence. Spasmodic bursts of devotion will not work. The more we understand and get to know God through our prayerful reading, the more we grow in love. Faithfulness to this communication with our divine Lover creates an ever-deepening intimacy with him. We come to know ourselves better, too, as we begin to see ourselves through the eyes of God. Gradually, lectio divina becomes a contemplative experience of love.

- *Expectation.* For the effective reception of lectio divina, we must trust that God is present and speaks to us through the inspired word. This type of personal trust in a God who cares about us deeply engenders expectation in the prayerful reader. If we believe that God is present in the word, we can be convinced that he is going to touch our lives. We expect that God will give us what he wants us to receive, working profoundly within our hearts and changing us at a deep level. God offers his word for a purpose, and his purpose will be effective to the degree that we anticipate being transformed by our loving God.

The word of God has the potential within it to nourish and transform us, just as healthful food contains everything needed to satisfy our bodily hungers and promote our vigorous development. But we must create the conditions for Scripture to do its work within us. When we cultivate these dispositions within ourselves, we allow the saving power within God's word to renovate our lives. Listen to the words of St. Bernard of Clairvaux (twelfth century), a Cistercian abbot and Father of the Church:

I store up the word of God as you would food. The word of God is a living bread, the food of the soul. Bread kept in a cupboard can be stolen, eaten by rats, go stale, but once it is eaten none of these misfortunes are to be feared. Store up the word of God like that, because blessed are those that keep it. Let it sink into your inmost heart and pass into your affections and way of life. Eat plentifully of it and your soul will rejoice. Never forget to eat this bread, lest your heart wither, but feed and strengthen it with so rich and fruitful a food. If you hold on to the Word, the Word will protect you. The Son of God will come to you and his Father also.[9]

Questions for Reflection or Discussion

1. The author says that the source of all genuine prayer is an interior desire for God. What is the origin of this desire? How do you experience this interior desire?

2. In what ways has the teaching of the Second Vatican Council, that "access to sacred Scripture ought to be widely available to the Christian faithful," been implemented in the last few decades?

3. What are some good reasons for reading the Bible? What is the best reason for biblical reading?

4. Why is it said that lectio divina has its roots in the Jewish tradition? What are the highlights of the growth of lectio divina in Christian history?

5. What characteristics of lectio divina seem most important to you?

6. Which of the necessary dispositions for lectio divina do you want to concentrate on in the immediate future?

Chapter Two

A Living Book, Centered in Christt

At the heart of lectio divina is the belief that the Scriptures are filled with God's Spirit, who continues to breathe life into them. The Bible is not just a collection of literature we have inherited from past ages. It is a living book, containing God's saving power. This text is just as effective today as when its inspired words were written by their authors in ancient times. Through the Holy Spirit, the words of the Bible can lead us into a personal encounter with Jesus Christ that can transform our lives. The Bible is not just hundreds of pages of paper and ink. It is the living word of God, and it can change us when we read it reflectively with open minds and hearts, under the guidance of God's Spirit.

The Indwelling of the Holy Spirit

The books of the Bible were written under the inspiration of the Holy Spirit. "Inspired" literally means "breathed in" by God. It is this breath of God, the Holy Spirit, acting through human authors, which makes these biblical words the living word of God.

Paul's second letter to Timothy declares the inspired power that God places in the sacred texts:

All scripture is inspired by God and is useful for teaching, for reproof, for correction, and for training in righteousness, so that everyone who belongs to God may be proficient, equipped for every good work. (2 Timothy 3:16-17)

God is the primary author of the entire Bible, both Old and New Testaments. We can trust that these sacred texts express his truth to us because they have been written under the Holy Spirit's inspiration.

The divinely revealed realities, which are contained and presented in the text of Sacred Scripture, have been written down under the inspiration of the Holy Spirit. For Holy Mother Church, relying on the faith of the apostolic age, accepts as sacred and canonical the books of the Old and the New Testaments, whole and entire, with all their parts, on the grounds that, written under the inspiration of the Holy Spirit (cf. John 20:31; 2 Timothy 3:16; 2 Peter 1:19-21; 3:15-16), they have God as their author and have been handed on as such to the Church herself. (*Dogmatic Constitution on Divine Revelation*, 11; see also *Catechism of the Catholic Church*, 105)

We limit our understanding of the Holy Spirit's work when we think of inspiration as something that happened only when the original authors wrote the biblical texts. Rather, the work of God's Spirit is an ongoing reality within the inspired books. The sacred texts remain inspired; they are always inspired; they are filled with the Spirit of God.

This understanding of the Spirit's enduring and ongoing presence in the text is essential for lectio divina. Through the Holy

Spirit, God is addressing his word to us here and now. Because of the indwelling Spirit, the word is alive and has the power to transform us. The word of God is charged with creative power to change and renew us.

"Just as the Spirit of life touched the spirit of the Prophet (biblical author), so he touches the spirit of the reader" (St. Gregory the Great, sixth century).[1] There is a deep spiritual union established between the human author of the text, who was moved by the Spirit to write, and the prayerful reader of the page, who is moved by that same Spirit when reading it. The difference in time does not matter, because both are joined to the living word animated through the same Holy Spirit.

The human authors of the Old and New Testaments are of course dead, and their work is finished. But as a living word, their text is penetrated by the life-giving Spirit whose work is never finished. St. Irenaeus (second century) said that the Spirit insures the Scriptures' perennial youth. The Spirit still speaks to us with vigor, making the living word of God present to us on every page. The Spirit continues to breathe power and life into the text, so that we can truly encounter there the living God as we pore over every page.

St. Jerome (fourth century) wrote that the Bible must be read and interpreted "in the light of the same Spirit by whom it was written."[2] Because of this ever-present divine Spirit, the sacred text is transformed from simple paper and ink to the illuminated page. When we reflectively ponder the text, we too can be transformed as we are enlightened by the same Holy Spirit.

The first Christian disciples realized that they did not have the human ability to understand everything that God had revealed to them in Jesus. Through the work of the Holy Spirit, they experienced an ever-deepening clarification of the word. This is the work of the "Spirit of truth," of which Jesus promised, "He will guide you into all the truth" (John 16:13). As disciples of Jesus today, we can trust in this promise and know that the Spirit will continue to guide us as we listen to God's word with openheartedness, reverence, faithfulness, and expectation.

Before our sacred reading of the biblical text, we should always invoke the Holy Spirit in prayer. We can call upon God's Spirit to breathe within us, to give us inspiration, and to guide us as we read. With trusting confidence, we can expect the following things to happen:

- *The Holy Spirit enables us to experience the Bible as God's living word.* In addition to studying the text's background and the meaning the human author was trying to convey through it, we can read Scripture as God's communication to us. Invoking God's Spirit enables us to interpret the Bible in a personal way and understand it as a personal word to us.

- *The Holy Spirit guides us toward a deeper understanding of the meaning of the Scriptures.* God's Spirit does not replace our own efforts to comprehend the Scriptures, but rather shows us the way to perceive his truth. The Holy Spirit begins by opening our minds, then gradually enables us to grasp the meaning that God wants to communicate for the growth of our faith and love.

- *The Holy Spirit motivates our response to God's word.*
  The Spirit works within us to allow what we read to affect
  our hearts and to gradually change our lives. Reading the
  Bible with God's Spirit active within us will not allow us
  to remain complacent, but will impel us to respond in
  some way. This response will be different for each of us,
  but the Holy Spirit will create a connection between what
  we read reflectively and our daily walk with Christ.

When we are not sincerely open and docile to the movements of
the Holy Spirit, we can easily begin to force our own private and
distorted meanings on the Bible. But when we humbly open our
lives to what God wants us to receive from Scripture, reading "in
the light of the same Spirit by whom it was written" as St. Jerome
recommended, we will experience the Bible as a living book and
be guided to understand and respond in the Holy Spirit.

Images of the Sacred Page

The theologians and spiritual writers of the early centuries saw
beneath the surface of the biblical page to the mysterious presence of God within. They knew Scripture as a source of saving
knowledge, as the word of God capable of transforming them,
and they knew that its readers would encounter him there.

These scholars expressed their deep love for the *sacra pagina*
in numerous ways. Because of their profound devotion, they
meticulously copied the pages of Scripture onto fine parchment
to preserve and disseminate the holy text. In the scriptoriums,
or copy rooms, of their monasteries, they illuminated the sacred
pages with gold leaf, brilliant colors, and exquisite miniature art.

They formed each letter as an act of devotion to the word of God, and they expressed the meaning of sacred Scripture in a variety of images. They saw the Bible as

- *A lamp to light our path.* As we walk in the darkness of this world, the holy text illuminates our way. With this light we can see the way he has marked out for us.

- *A letter written to us by God.* In this divine love letter, God has communicated to us in a most intimate way and revealed to us his secrets. His personal message is addressed to us to read and cherish.

- *A sea of deep mysteries.* The Scriptures are an unfathomable sea upon which we enter with our fragile boat. Origen wrote, "Just as one who goes to sea in a small boat feels extremely anxious about entrusting a small vessel to such huge waves, so we too suffer when we dare to penetrate such a great sea of mysteries."[3]

- *A table set for us by God.* At the table of his word, God offers us the choicest of delicious and nourishing food. Here he feeds our spirits for the journey ahead and refreshes us with his delights.

- *A deep well full of refreshing water.* No matter how many times we dip into the well of sacred Scripture, there is always more quenching water to drink. God's word never goes stale but always refreshes our weary spirits.

The One Book That Is Christ

From the earliest days of the church, the community of disciples has always read the Old Testament from the perspective of Christ. He himself completes and fulfills the expectations and promises of the old covenant. In fact, Jesus taught his disciples to see the rich continuity in God's plan of salvation and to appreciate how all of salvation history pointed to his coming. As the two disciples traveled with the risen Lord on the road to Emmaus, he demonstrated this method of understanding the Hebrew Scriptures: "Then beginning with Moses and all the prophets, he interpreted to them the things about himself in all the scriptures" (Luke 24:27).

Of course the Hebrew Scriptures have value in and of themselves. We can read them as the fascinating story of God's relationship with the people of Israel. Likewise, we can read the New Testament alone, as the story of Jesus and the early church. But for the Christian believer, the two testaments form one book, one chronicle of God's saving plan for the world. The mystery of Christ is the focal center of the entire Bible.

Reading both testaments as an integral whole enriches our understanding of each part and deepens our perception of God. St. Augustine (fifth century) expressed this critical relationship between the two parts of Scripture: "The New Testament lies hidden in the Old, and the Old Testament is unveiled in the New."[4] We cannot fully understand one testament without the other, because only together do they express God's full revelation. As Christians we understand the Old Testament fully only when we see it as a mother who bears the New Testament in her womb and gives birth to it.

In the Gospel of John, Jesus taught his persecutors that the Old Testament Scriptures are a veiled and prophetic witness to himself. To those who accused him of blasphemy, he responded, "You search the scriptures because you think that in them you have eternal life; and it is they that testify on my behalf" (John 5:39). He said further, "If you believed Moses, you would believe me, for he wrote about me" (John 5:46). He knew that those who placed their faith in him would come to see that the texts of the old covenant receive their fulfillment in him. Eventually, they would come to recognize his presence throughout the Scriptures.

Through the work of the Holy Spirit within us, we can see Christ whenever we read a page of sacred Scripture. This is the heart of lectio divina—to see Christ everywhere in God's word. With this understanding, the prayerful reader can perceive the ultimate purpose of Scripture and realize its unity. As Hugh of St. Victor (twelfth century) tells us so beautifully,

> All Sacred Scripture is but one book, and this one book is Christ; because all sacred Scripture speaks of Christ, and all sacred Scripture is fulfilled in Christ.[5]

The Word, Abbreviated and Concentrated

In his divine eternity, God has spoken only one Word: "In the beginning was the Word, and the Word was with God, and the Word was God" (John 1:1). However, before Jesus came, that word expressed itself in many different ways. It was multiplied through the diverse language of the Old Testament Scriptures. God communicated his message of salvation to us in various and partial ways through the voices of many inspired writers.

But when the fullness of time came, the Word returned to its original unity: "The Word became flesh and lived among us" (John 1:14). Now God speaks to us through Christ:

> Long ago God spoke to our ancestors in many and various ways by the prophets, but in these last days he has spoken to us by a Son, whom he appointed heir of all things. (Hebrews 1:1-2)

The many words became the one Word, the living Word to which every other word bears witness. As St. Augustine (fifth century) said, "Earlier times were granted the prophets who were inspired and filled with the word of God; we have been granted the Word of God himself as prophet."[6]

God's Word is now not only audible but visible and tangible, now not only spoken but incarnate and living. Like John, we too can say that we have received a personal revelation of Jesus, the Word who has now become our eternal life:

> We declare to you what was from the beginning, what we have heard, what we have seen with our eyes, what we have looked at and touched with our hands, concerning the word of life—this life was revealed, and we have seen it and testify to it, and declare to you the eternal life that was with the Father and was revealed to us—we declare to you what we have seen and heard so that you also may have fellowship with us; and truly our fellowship is with the Father and with his Son Jesus Christ. (1 John 1:1-3)

When we prayerfully read the Scriptures, we remind ourselves that we are hearing echoes of the Word who is now alive in us, the Word who was God and was with God "in the beginning." This is the Word that God expressed in the Spirit before it was written down in inspired texts. He is the Word that God sent to be the light and life of all people.

St. Augustine (fifth century) explains that God speaks this one Word through all the words of Scripture. Through this one eternal Utterance, God expresses himself completely:

> You recall that one and the same Word of God extends throughout Scripture, that it is one and the same Utterance that resounds in the mouths of all the sacred writers, since he who was in the beginning God with God has no need of separate syllables; for he is not subject to time.[7]

The Christian who reads the Bible in faith always finds Christ at the heart of the text. This is true for both the Old and the New Testaments. To prayerfully read the Scriptures is to listen to Christ speaking to us. Christ reveals the ultimate meaning of God's revelation, and all of God's saving plan is condensed in the one Word that is Christ.

Christ, the Word made flesh, has traditionally been called the *Verbum abbreviatum*, the "abbreviated Word." The entire Bible finds its unity in him. In Christ, the many parts of the Bible are harmonized and perfected. The one Word condenses all of Scripture into a summary that brings salvation. John of the Cross (sixteenth century) put it succinctly in *The Ascent of Mount Carmel*: "In giving us his Son, who is his only Word, God has said everything to us at once, in one single stroke, in this single word—and he has nothing more to say."[8]

Lectio divina, then, is not so much a matter of interpreting a book as of seeking Someone. It is the church seeking its beloved Christ. The meaning we find in the Scriptures is not impersonal truth but ultimately the person of Christ. For this reason, reflecting on sacred texts becomes not primarily an intellectual exercise but a devoted and passionate search, an enthusiastic and joyful discovery.

Searching for the personal communication of Christ to us in prayerful reading is like the bride's search for her beloved in the Song of Songs. The ardent and relentless quest expressed in these love poems is a wonderful metaphor used by the ancient writers for lectio divina. "If you pray, you are speaking to your Spouse; if you read, he is speaking to you" (St. Jerome, fourth century).[9] The devoted dialogue of prayerful reading leads to an experience of the soul aglow with divine love. "The thirsty soul eagerly prolongs its contact with Scripture, certain to find there the One for whom it thirsts" (St. Bernard of Clairvaux, twelfth century).[10]

The Great Sacrament of Scripture

One way to explore the living power of sacred Scripture is to reflect on its sacramental nature. A sacrament is a material element that contains and communicates a divine reality. In this sense, when the Word became flesh, Christ became the "primordial sacrament" (Origen, third century). In him, the idea of a sacrament is fully expressed. We encounter God through Christ's humanity, through his physical nature. The seven sacraments of the church continue to express Christ by communicating his saving presence through visible and tangible signs. Every element of the church's liturgy looks beyond these signs to the living presence of Christ.

The ancients understood Scripture as a great sacrament. Through the material signs of the Bible—its sacred text, its inspired literature, and the events recorded there—it presents to us an invisible, divine reality. The material wrapping of the Bible contains the mystery of our salvation. When we go beneath the letter of Scripture to the mystery within, we encounter Christ at the center. Sacred Scripture is the sacrament of our encounter with Jesus Christ.

The master key that unlocks all the mysteries of Scripture is the cross. When Christ died on the cross, the gospels tell us that the veil concealing the presence of God in the temple was torn from top to bottom. Likewise, God's plan for our redemption, which was concealed within all the texts of Scripture, was unveiled through Christ's self-offering to the Father. Through the cross, the Holy Spirit opened the eyes and the hearts of God's people so they could experience Scripture as a great sacrament revealing Christ.

In this sense, the Scriptures are much like the Eucharist. The patristic writers make this parallel frequently, declaring that they are as a loaf of bread in Christ's hands. Just as the eucharistic consecration turns ordinary bread into Christ's body, his offering on the cross transforms Scripture into the living Word. Both are the bread of life; both give spiritual nourishment to God's people.

Listening to Scripture, just as receiving Eucharist, is meant to be an expectant experience of divine glory, an anticipation of the kingdom of God. As St. Jerome (fourth century) reminds us, Scripture is a vital part of our Christian life:

> Since the Lord's flesh is real food and his blood real drink . . . our only good in the present age is to eat his flesh and drink his blood, not only in the eucharistic mystery but also in the reading of Scripture.[11]

In the liturgy of the church, we venerate Christ's presence in Scripture just as we venerate his presence in the Eucharist. We often bring candles and incense to the ambo where the Scriptures are proclaimed, as well as to the altar. The ordained minister bows, crosses himself, and kisses the book—gestures of reverence signifying that Christ is present in the gospels as well as at the sacrament of the altar.

Our recent teachings also express the unity of the word of God and the body of Christ as living bread for God's people:

> The Church has always venerated the divine Scriptures just as she venerated the Body of the Lord, in so far as she never ceases, particularly in the sacred liturgy, to partake of the bread of life and to offer it to the faithful from the one table of the Word of God and the Body of Christ. (*Dogmatic Constitution on Divine Revelation*, 21; see also *Catechism of the Catholic Church*, 103)

Of course, God does not operate through the liturgy alone. Just as we should maintain a balance between liturgical prayer and private prayer, we should also try to read his word in private, as well as to hear it proclaimed in public. For as Christ is present in the Scriptures proclaimed in liturgy, so, too, he is present when we prayerfully reflect on them in silent meditation. When we read the Bible expecting that Jesus will speak to our lives and nourish us with his presence, we will be changed and renewed. Just as the sacraments affect our lives when we open ourselves to the grace shared with us in those sacred moments, so too, the Scriptures can transform us when we read them with open hearts.

God addresses the community of his people in the Liturgy of the Word, and he addresses us personally in lectio divina. But we don't need to focus on one at the expense of the other. In fact, lectio divina is the natural complement of liturgical proclamation: if we are receptive, our personal Scripture reading will enhance our liturgical hearing, and vice-versa. The insights we gain from silent contemplation of Scripture will become magnified during the liturgy. Likewise, we will remember inspiring words from the liturgy during our private prayer, as we enter more deeply into communion with God.

The Life-changing Power of God's Word

When we read the Bible as the word of God, it becomes a personal communication with us here and now. Sometimes that word is comforting and consoling; at other times it is severe and challenging. But whether gentle or harsh, the Scriptures always call us to face God and to confront ourselves. When we read the Bible as a living book for people of faith, then we must begin a dialogue with God and become personally involved. We cannot escape without a response.

In the biblical tradition, the term "word of God" describes God's self-revelation. His word is powerful because it is so much more than a word—it communicates his healing strength and his saving authority. When we receive his word into our lives, we can expect to be changed.

Here are some of the biblical images that express the transforming power of the divine word:

- *"The grass withers, the flower fades; but the word of our God will stand forever"* (Isaiah 40:8). In our world where words are cheap and fleeting, we can trust that God's word is permanently valid and our source of unchanging truth. The word of our God will stand forever, as all else passes away.

- *"Is not my word like fire, says the LORD, and like a hammer that breaks a rock in pieces?"* (Jeremiah 23:29). The voice of God speaking in our lives is an intense and penetrating fire, an announcement that shatters our conventional ideas and comfortable ways of thinking.

- *"The word of God is living and active, sharper than any two-edged sword, piercing until it divides soul from spirit, joints from marrow; it is able to judge the thoughts and intentions of the heart"* (Hebrews 4:12). Like a piercing sword, God's word penetrates into the deepest parts of our being. Everything about us is laid bare, and nothing can remain hidden from God's penetrating power.

- *"Your word is a lamp to my feet and a light to my path"* (Psalm 119:105). God's word becomes a luminous beacon that guides our way through life's darkness. Our path becomes illumined by a guiding truth that shows us the way.

- *"The sower sows the word. . . . And these are the ones sown on the good soil: they hear the word and accept it and bear fruit, thirty and sixty and a hundredfold"* (Mark 4:14, 20). The word of God can bring about true conversion when we cultivate it in our hearts and allow it to produce results within our lives.

When we prayerfully read the great living book of sacred Scripture, we cannot remain the same. The more we remove the obstacles in our way—our impatience, fears, temptations, complacency, and misunderstandings—the more powerfully Scripture will change us. Sometimes these changes are overwhelming; often they are more subtle. We gradually become aware that the fruit of studying the Bible is the fruit of the Spirit: "love, joy, peace, patience, kindness, generosity, faithfulness, gentleness, and self-control" (Galatians 5:22-23). When we begin to notice this fruit in the midst of the way we live each day, we will know that the word of God is working within us.

Questions for Reflection or Discussion

1. What difference does it make that the biblical words are inspired by the Holy Spirit? In what way can you experience God's Spirit working in you through prayerful reading of the Bible?

2. Which of the images of Scripture, given to us by ancient Christian writers, most expresses your growing understanding of the sacred text?

3. What is your understanding of the words of St. Augustine in explaining the relationship between the Old and New Testaments? In what way can both testaments be considered by Christians as one book?

4. How can you read the Scriptures not only as a quest for intellectual meaning but as a search for Christ and a passionate discovery of him?

5. What is your understanding of Scripture as a great sacrament of our encounter with Christ? What is the relationship between lectio divina and the church's eucharistic liturgy?

6. Which of the biblical images of God's word best expresses its transforming potential for you? How does this image express the life-changing power of Scripture in your own life?

Chapter Three

Lectio: Reading the Text
with a Listening Ear

M any have mistakenly considered lectio divina as a highly specialized method of prayer, consisting of a series of steps that must be rigidly followed. Certainly, spiritual writers through the centuries have developed techniques and processes for sacred reading that can be helpful, especially for beginners. But it is important to say at the outset that lectio divina is not a methodical system. There are no obligatory steps, and the most fruitful exercise of lectio does not necessarily follow a required sequence or seek any specific goal.

The most important thing to keep in mind when practicing lectio divina is that it is meant to lead us to a personal encounter and dialogue with God. There is no need to anxiously assess the quality of our sacred reading as if we had to follow it "correctly" to achieve some particular target. There is no goal other than prayerfully reading Scripture in God's presence with a desire to deepen our heart-to-heart intimacy with him. In lectio divina we let go of our own agenda and gradually open ourselves to what God wants us to experience through the sacred page.

A Ladder or a Circle?

The description of lectio divina as an organized step-by-step system dates back to the twelfth century A.D.—a late date considering that a rich tradition of lectio divina had existed centuries earlier. It comes from a book written by Guigo II, a Carthusian monk, entitled *Scala Claustralium*, "The Monk's Ladder."[1] More than any other source, this treatise has given the world the distorted impression that lectio divina is a strict method consisting of four sequential steps for attaining union with God.

In his book, Guigo retains four terms used in the the earlier tradition of lectio divina: *lectio* (reading), *meditatio* (meditation), *oratio* (prayer), and *contemplatio* (contemplation). He describes these steps as four rungs on an ascending ladder, the lower end resting on the earth and the top reaching the heavens. On this ladder, he writes, monks are "lifted up from earth to heaven."[2]

Guigo tells us that these four stages are all rooted in reading sacred Scripture and are intimately connected. The stages are influenced by one another, and together they form a single development of the soul. Guigo uses a helpful image to give readers an understanding of how the stages relate to one another:

> Reading, as it were, puts food whole into the mouth, meditation chews it and breaks it up, prayer extracts its flavor, contemplation is the sweetness itself which gladdens and refreshes.[3]

Guigo claims, "The first degree (*lectio*) is proper for beginners, the second (*meditatio*) to proficients, the third (*oratio*) to devotees, the fourth (*contemplatio*) to the blessed."[4] As the influence of his writing grew, scholars began to see the steps as a hierarchical process not meant for ordinary people. The higher rungs of the ladder, especially contemplation, were reserved for those who had special graces. Contemplation was identified with extraordinary mystical states, something to be admired from a safe distance by laypeople. Lamentably, this analytical and categorical approach to lectio divina is far different from the practice developed in the early church and is one of the primary reasons why lectio disappeared from the church's life for so many centuries.

The desert fathers and monks who began the tradition of lectio distrusted methods of prayer and spiritual practice that were too rigidly defined. They knew that sacred Scripture affects us in many different ways. Sometimes these effects may happen simultaneously, or they may blend together. They understood that we need a certain amount of spontaneous freedom to relate to God's Spirit. The terms they used to describe lectio divina were meant to be interrelated: *lectio* (reading), *cogitatio* (reflection), *studium* (study), *meditatio* (meditation), *oratio* (prayer), and *contemplatio* (contemplation).

Contemporary writers who are trying to revive lectio divina tend to move away from categorical descriptions of the practice and return us to its earlier roots. The Trappist monk Thomas Keating uses the same terms as Guigo to describe lectio divina: reading, meditation, prayer, and contemplation. However, he pictures them as four moments along the circumference of a circle.[5] Another Trappist monk, Basil Pennington, adds two terms to this circular practice: *compassio* (compassion) and *operatio* (action).[6]

From both of these perspectives, there are no stages, steps, or ladders to lectio divina. All the moments of the circle are joined to one another as well as to the center, which is God's Spirit speaking to our hearts through the biblical text. The practice may begin at any moment along the circle and may move gently from one moment to another as the Spirit moves us. This is a process that is available to all God's people and certainly does not require any unusual graces or extraordinary holiness.

Lectio divina essentially describes a way of developing a love relationship with God. There are no "methods" for growing in love, yet there are certain moments that are common to all intimate relationships. Basil Pennington describes lectio divina as "a way of friendship" with the Lord. Friendship blossoms when one becomes more fully acquainted with the other, and this personal connection leads to growing trust.

Pennington names the four moments of this "way of friendship" as acquaintanceship, friendly companionship, friendship, and union.[7] This is the type of relationship Jesus desires with his disciples: "I have called you friends, because I have made known to you everything that I have heard from my Father" (John 15:15). Another spiritual writer, Thelma Hall, RC, also uses this analogy of an intimate relationship. She says that our loving intimacy with God grows through a continuum of knowing, trusting, desiring, and then surrendering our defenses and fears, and ultimately our very selves, to the Beloved.[8] These phases correspond to the progressive stages of lectio divina.

Writers use a variety of terms to describe the process of lectio divina: steps, stages, degrees, elements, phases, moments, and others. Each of these words expresses some aspect of the traditional practice. All of them have their value, but none of them are ideal. The term I use most frequently throughout my work is "movement." Like the various movements in a classical work of music, the phases of lectio divina each have their own characteristics and can even be practiced independently of one another. Yet, for the complete experience of lectio divina, all of the movements are necessary.

My own analysis of the tradition includes five movements: lectio, meditatio, oratio, contemplatio, and operatio, though a number of other movements from various spiritual traditions may be incorporated within these five. The term "movement" avoids any accent on a hierarchical step-by-step procedure and emphasizes that everyone experiences the practice in a unique way. There is plenty of room for personal interpretation of each movement in the exercise of lectio divina.

Listening with the Ear of Our Hearts

All descriptions of lectio divina are based on the first movement: lectio—reading the text of sacred Scripture. This is the foundation of the entire tradition, and it is clearly the most important step in the process. That is why we should approach our reading of Scripture reverently and expectantly, knowing that if we do so, the Holy Spirit will connect us to the inspired word in a personal way.

Our Bible should be one of our most treasured possessions. We know that it represents a divine presence, a place where we can truly encounter our faithful God. We want to keep our Bible in a special and honored location. Many people have the practice of enthroning the Scriptures on a bookstand in their living room, bedroom, or office. Our Bible is likely not a beautifully illuminated manuscript, but every Bible is sacred, because in its pages we can receive divine revelation. Treating our Bible with reverence is a tangible reminder that we are dealing with a book that holds the mystery of God.

Before we begin to read, we may want to hold our Bible respectfully in our hands and thank God for the gift of his word. We can then turn to the Holy Spirit, who inspired the text we are about to read, and who abides today with us. We pray that God's Spirit will enable us to experience our Bible as a living book and help us understand what he wants to personally communicate with us. Some small ritual for invoking the divine presence, such as lighting a candle or kissing the biblical page, will help set this time and space apart for an encounter with God.

We should always keep in mind that lectio is not just ordinary reading. It might best be described as listening deeply— what Benedict (sixth century) described in his community rule as hearing "with the ear of our hearts."[9] In lectio, God speaks and I listen.

On our part, this listening requires that we do our best to receive God's word with as little prejudgment as possible, as if we were hearing it for the first time. Though we may find it difficult to step out of our "comfort zone," we cannot listen fully to God if we think we already know what the text is going to tell us. We don't want to reduce divine communication to the narrow confines of our own ideas and expectations. Rather, lectio requires that we create a space within us for the new wisdom and understanding God wants to give us through the sacred page.

This kind of hearing requires fully attentive reading. However, one of the consequences of this information age is that our culture is drowned in written words. We tend to read in a hurry, curious to learn more and more. But lectio cannot be hasty. We must read for understanding and assimilation. Ambrose (fourth century) reached out to our modern era when he wrote, "We should read not in agitation, but in calm; not hurriedly, but slowly, a few words at a time, pausing in attentive reflection. . . . Then the reader will experience their ability to enkindle the ardor of prayer."[10]

In order to instill in ourselves the sense that reading Scripture is a deep listening, we might consider returning to the practice of reading it aloud. In the ancient world, where books were precious and rare, people listened to their sacred texts by hearing them read aloud. This type of hearing required full attention and careful listening. But even when reading was done in private, reading aloud was the usual practice. The words were always pronounced vocally; thus, the text was seen with the eyes and heard with the ear. Both the sight and the sound of the words allowed for easier comprehension and memorization. This traditional practice is continued in synagogues today, as Jewish believers not only read their Scriptures but pronounce them aloud and often move their bodies rhythmically as they take them to heart.

For us as well as for our ancestors in the faith, the eyes and ears and even the mind are not the word's final destination. We listen to the sacred text so that the words of Scripture might finally reside in our hearts. There we are capable of reflecting on their insights, messages, and inspirations in a way that can radically transform our lives.

What Does This Text Say?

The essential question to ask in this first movement (lectio) is, "What does this text say?" Further questions we can ask in the later movements of lectio divina are, "What does this text say to me?" "What do I want to say to God after reading this text?" and "What difference does this text make in my life?" But the basic task of lectio is to focus on the sacred page itself as it is presented to us in the Scriptures.

First of all, we can read the text as literature—looking at its words, images, and characters. We can look at its structure and its literary form—is it poetry, parable, history, proverb, legal code, epic, or apocalypse? We should realize that God's truth is expressed in a variety of types of literature, each type expressing inspired truth in a different way. A good biblical commentary or study Bible can be of considerable help at this stage.

Our primary concern here is to understand the meaning that the original authors intended to express. We will be able to probe all the potential that the text can offer us the more we comprehend something of the original context—historical, cultural, geographical, literary, and religious. When, where, and why was the author writing? Furthermore, we must ask, "How does the writer's faith manifest itself in the text?" and "What kind of faith response does the writer expect from the reader?" Emphasizing the faith dimension of the text helps us transcend the original circumstances in which it was written and allows us to see the lasting significance and validity it has for all of us.

There is nothing wrong with including the results of good biblical scholarship in our lectio. The Jewish rabbinical tradition teaches us how artificial it is to try to make a clear distinction between study of Scripture and its prayerful reading. St. Jerome (fourth century) insisted on the harmony between biblical scholarship and contemplation. Study and lectio are not opposed; rather, we must integrate them. Yet, neither is an end in itself. We should always orient our reading and study toward prayerful reflection, in order to fully experience the grace of God's word.

The Past and Present Meanings of Biblical Texts

The original meaning of a biblical text is called its "literal sense." In order to properly interpret a scriptural text, any new insight we can gain into it must be based on this literal sense. This helps to assure that our interpretation is authentic and not overly subjective or speculative.

However, in addition to the original meaning of a text, there are a variety of other meanings present within it. In the work of biblical interpretation, our first task is to determine what the text *meant*, but further study seeks to speculate about what the text *means*. Both the original meaning and fuller contemporary meanings are legitimate quests for biblical study.

The Pontifical Biblical Commission has taught that, in addition to searching for the original meaning of the text, biblical scholarship must seek further meaning as the text is interpreted as the word of God. The commission wrote that interpretation "should also explain the Christological, canonical, and ecclesial meanings of the biblical texts."[11]

The "Christological meaning" of a text is the deeper significance it has for us when we read it in the light of Christ. Since the mystery of Christ is the focus of all Scripture, texts are enriched with new meaning when we read them under the influence of the Holy Spirit, in the context of the mystery of Jesus Christ.

"Canonical meaning" is the additional meaning we find within an individual text when we read it in the context of the entire Bible. Individual texts written at different stages of salvation history impact us more profoundly when we can see their place within the biblical tradition.

"Ecclesial meaning" is the fuller meaning we see in a text when we understand it within the living tradition of the church. Since the biblical texts developed as part of the believing communities of Israel and the early church, the Bible is most fully understood through the lens of the community that shaped it and continues to nourish it. So Christians can view this ecclesial aspect of Scripture as God speaking his word to the church, the guiding and challenging word he still uses today to shape his people.

These three types of meaning build on the literal sense of the Scriptural text, but they go beyond the literal sense. Generally the biblical authors could not envision these fuller dimensions of the texts at the time they wrote them. Yet these factors are inherent in the texts and are part of their inspired meaning. Since the divine author intended the Scriptures for the wider understanding of the church through the centuries, their significance continually unfolds for us as we read them in the larger context of his plan of salvation.

Because the Pontifical Biblical Commission urges scholars to delve into these further meanings of Scripture, we can expect biblical commentaries to offer a richer explanation of these dimensions. When choosing a commentary, look for works that discuss these further meanings. For example, search for Old Testament commentaries that not only explore passages in the context of ancient Israel but also examine them in the light of Christ. Look for commentaries that relate texts to other books of the Bible, shedding further light on their significance in the canon of Scripture. Search also for commentaries that offer interpretations by the early theologians of the church, such as Irenaeus, Origen, Jerome, and Augustine. These commentaries can help us understand the multilayered meanings within the Scriptures and enrich our hearing of the inspired word.

A Divine and Human Word

Modern biblical scholarship has given us wonderful means for understanding Scripture in ways not possible in earlier times. Historical studies can tell us a great deal about how a passage developed, its original sources, and the methods editors used to create the complete text by combining their sources in unique ways. All of these studies help us understand the intentions of the human authors and the process by which they arrived at the final versions of the sacred texts that have been handed down to us.

Through the use of scientific research methods, we recognize ever more clearly that the language of the Bible was conditioned by the time and culture in which it was written. The Scriptures were composed by human authors in particular times and circumstances, with all the limitations and historical peculiarities that are characteristic of literature.

One reaction to contemporary biblical scholarship has been the emergence of biblical fundamentalism, which continues to grow in influence. Fundamentalism refuses to take into account the historical character of the Bible's revelation and rejects many modern methods of biblical interpretation. By treating the biblical text as if the Holy Spirit had dictated it word for word, fundamentalism refuses to admit that the inspired word of God was written in human language by authors possessing limited understanding. It fails to recognize that the inspired text was steeped in the language and culture of its time. In short, fundamentalism does not accept the human character of the sacred Scriptures.

In order to avoid both the sterile rationalism of approaching the Bible as a purely human document and the simplicity of the fundamentalist approach, we must understand the "incarnational" nature of the sacred texts: the Bible is the word of God, written in the words of human beings. Just as Jesus is fully God and fully human, so the Scriptures are both divine and human:

> Indeed the words of God, expressed in the words of men, are in every way like human language, just as the Word of the eternal Father, when he took on himself the flesh of human weakness, became like men. (*Dogmatic Constitution on Divine Revelation*, 13; see also *Catechism of the Catholic Church*, 101)

A text that God had miraculously dictated to humans from on high might be easier to believe than a word written by human beings over many centuries. In the same way, a God who descended to earth amidst spectacular wonders might be easier to believe than a God who came in human flesh, living in poverty and suffering. When we listen to the word of God in Scripture, we must realize the full humanity of that word. Jesus is the Word made flesh; the Bible is the word of God in human words. We will not understand the Scriptures completely if we undervalue either their full divinity or their full humanity.

We can better appreciate this incarnational understanding of Scripture if we think about how God inspired its human authors. He guided them so that they communicated the truth he wanted to entrust to the Bible. But while guiding them, he did not violate their freedom: he did not prevent them from expressing their own individual personalities and viewpoints. God gave these human authors understanding, insight, wisdom, and the impulse to write but left them free to think, to choose, and to express ideas in their own unique way.

> To compose the sacred books, God chose certain men who, all the while he employed them in this task, made full use of their powers and faculties so that, though he acted in them and by them, it was as true authors that they consigned to writing whatever he wanted written, and no more. (*Dogmatic Constitution on Divine Revelation*, 11; see also *Catechism of the Catholic Church*, 106)

So we see how profoundly the Bible is the product of both God and human beings. This means that the message of salvation comes to us through human history. It means that the revelation of God is communicated through the diverse literary styles of humanity. It means that the truth God revealed in Scripture is totally reliable, but that the manner in which that truth is revealed is less than the perfection of God. It means that the treasure of revelation comes to us in earthen vessels (2 Corinthians 4:7).

The understanding that God is the primary author of the Bible assures readers that the biblical texts are God's word for all time. Because the Bible is inspired by God, we can have absolute confidence that the limitations of its human authors do not distort the saving truth that he teaches us through his word.

Lectio in the Life of Mary

Mary learned to listen to the word of God in the Jewish tradition. As a child, she learned the Hebrew Scriptures from her parents, and the words of those texts resonated in her mind and heart as she matured. In the temple at Jerusalem and the synagogue at Nazareth she heard the word of God, chanted it, and sought to live according to its guidance.

The traditional icons of the annunciation always depict Mary reading the text of Scripture. This attentive listening to the divine word prepared her to receive the new divine revelation brought by the angel Gabriel. In fact, the icons portray her continuing her reading as Gabriel proclaimed the good news to her, as if the announcement were a continuation of what she was already reading. In time, she would see that those sacred texts were fulfilled in her own life and in that of her Son.

Mary's whole life with Jesus, from Nazareth to Cana to Jerusalem, was a careful reading of the Word, an attentive listening to the Word, in an increasingly intimate and incarnate sense. As the woman of the word, Mary teaches us how to pray the lectio with receptive and expectant devotion.

Questions for Reflection or Discussion

1. Why are the various movements of lectio divina best described as a circle rather than a ladder? What are the risks of viewing lectio divina as a ladder reaching into heaven?

2. How do the phases of lectio divina compare with your experience of growing in a close relationship with another?

3. What is the difference between lectio and our ordinary reading? What difference does it make when you "listen with the ears of your heart"?

4. Why is it important to first understand the literary form of a text and the intention of its original human author? Why should these elements matter so much if the text is the word of God?

5. In what way can biblical texts contain "fuller meanings" in addition to the meaning intended by the original human author?

6. Why is it so critical to understand both the divine and the human characteristics of the Bible in order to avoid the simplicity of fundamentalism?

Meditatio: Reflecting on the Meaning and Message of the Text

While the first movement (*lectio*) asks the question, "What does this text say?" the next movement (*meditatio*) asks the further question, "What does this text say to *me*?" Meditatio aims to bring the text into the sphere of my own life, seeking to understand what the Scripture passage says to me today. It focuses on the lasting purpose of the sacred page, transcending the text's original setting by reflecting on its faith dimension.

Preparing for Meditation

Reading the Bible is a challenge, because when we do so we encounter a wall that divides the text of the past from our lives today. That wall is created by the difference in time, language, culture, and experience between the world in which the Bible was written and our own contemporary world. The challenge for those who wish to prayerfully reflect on the Scriptures today is to bridge the gap between these two worlds.

When the patristic writers of the early church interpreted the Bible, they considered their work satisfactory only when they had found a meaning in the text that was relevant to the situation of Christians in their own day. This is the work of meditatio. We must link the biblical truth contained in the Scriptures to the experience of faith in the world we live in.

By meditating on the text, we begin to break down the wall between the sacred page, written so long ago, and our own lives today. In this way we can create a dialogue with God. This break in the wall is created in two ways. First, we penetrate the wall through listening attentively to the text, and second, through reflecting on our own experience. We can create the conditions for meditatio when we establish connections between the text of yesterday and the today of our lives.

One link between the distant past and our modern world comes with the realization that human nature is essentially the same in every time and place. The basic questions and struggles of our lives are very similar to those faced by people in biblical times. All of us have basic spiritual needs and struggles, and we all desire to reach out to God. In this way, the Bible is not just an ancient book; it is also a contemporary book that speaks to our present reality.

Because God is the primary author of Scripture, he can speak to the present through the scriptural record of the past. As the word of God, the Bible has a richness of meaning that can be discovered by every age and every culture. It has a particular message that can be received by every reader who listens to God's word in the context of his or her daily experiences.

It is often difficult to know when we pass from lectio to meditatio and to discern the signs that mark that passage. But we should read a text until it becomes like a mirror, reflecting some of our own experiences, challenges, thoughts, and questions. In this way the sacred page gradually becomes our own word. We know that lectio is being transformed into meditatio when we come to realize that God is trying to speak personally to us and offer us a message through the scriptural text.

Letting the Word Resound within Us

After hearing a work of music that has moved us, we naturally want to reflect upon it, letting it echo within us. After reading a poem that strikes us deeply, we want to pause in silence to allow it to resonate and complete its work in us. This should be our response to the sacred text when we allow Christ to speak to us and guide us through his Spirit. We want to create a space in our hearts for God's word to reside. To practice meditatio well is to let the Scriptures take root in us, penetrating the deepest part of our being so that they become part of us.

The more we meditate on God's word, the more it grows within us, molding our thoughts, our feelings, and our lives. St. Ambrose (fourth century) described how this assimilation takes place: "When we drink from sacred Scripture, the life-sap of the eternal Word penetrates the veins of our soul and our inner faculties."[1] The purpose of meditatio is to allow the dynamic word of God to so penetrate our lives that it truly dwells within us and we begin to embody its truth and its love.

We know by faith that the inspired text has the potential to transform us, just as it did our ancestors. Even though it was written centuries ago, it still has a message for us. This message is what we seek in meditatio. We find it by reflecting on the text, dialoguing with it, and allowing it into the sphere of our own lives. Guigo (twelfth century) describes meditatio as the process of seeking this message through our own reflection: "*Meditatio* is the intellect's careful activity that with the help of its own insight searches for the knowledge of the hidden truth."[2]

To find this "hidden truth," we must listen for what the Scripture text is saying to us, what it may be offering us, and what it may be demanding of us. This interior understanding is always present to us, lying beneath the surface of the Scriptures. Once we grasp this truth with the mind, we must let it descend to the heart where we can assimilate it more deeply. There the difference between the word of God and our own word is less clear; the distinction between Scripture and our own life is less distinct. When we allow the sacred text to penetrate our minds and our hearts, we have begun to truly embody the *sacra pagina*.

Ruminating on the Text

In the prophetic writing of Ezekiel, we see a simple but profound illustration of what happens when we obediently and receptively take the word of God within us:

> He said to me, O mortal, eat what is offered to you; eat this scroll, and go, speak to the house of Israel. So I opened my mouth, and he gave me the scroll to eat. He said to me, Mortal, eat this scroll that I give you and fill your stomach with it. Then I ate it; and in my mouth it was as sweet as honey. (Ezekiel 3:1-3)

By pondering the words of Scripture, as Ezekiel did, we taste their sweetness, understand their personal meaning for us, imprint them in our memories, and relish them in our hearts. In this way the Scriptures become the basic food of our spiritual life.

Meditatio has been aptly referred to as the "chewing" of Scripture's "sweet and nourishing food" (St. Augustine). Only by slowly chewing this holy food can we savor it, digest it, and absorb it into our whole being. The tradition refers to this chewing as "rumination," a word which originally described the way a cow chews its cud. The animal's slow, repeated chewing to ensure thorough digestion describes the method of unhurriedly repeating a scriptural text with the intention of making it one's own.

A worthwhile way of "feeding" on Scripture is to choose a sentence or phrase of the text that speaks to us personally, then spend time meditating on it. We can gently repeat it, taking it to heart, and allow it to interact with our thoughts, feelings, memories, hopes, and desires. As we repeat the passage slowly, over and over, we will receive new insight and understanding.

Through this unhurried ruminating, God's word will begin to affect us at increasingly deeper levels. St. Gregory the Great (sixth century) said that without any great effort on our part, but simply by allowing the Spirit to act on us, meditatio opens the way for the Lord to enter into our hearts and enflame them with the grace of his love.

Using Questions for Reflection

Sometimes the best way to meditate on a scriptural passage is to ask questions of the text. Some questions will help us make connections between the world of the text and our own experience: "What aspects of the biblical world resemble our situation today?" "What aspects of our present condition does the text seem to address?" "What is the text's message for us right now?"

Other questions help us focus on more personal aspects of the text that we might want to reflect on in a deeper way: "What emotions and memories does this passage evoke within me?" "Where do I hear Christ speaking to me most personally in these verses?" "What grace is this text offering me?" "Which phrase do I want to bring with me to recall throughout the day?"

Often we will notice that rather than our questioning the Scriptures, they are questioning us. The text will challenge us to go beyond our current level of comfort and security: "What attitudes or habits must I change in order to truly live out these inspired words?" "Why am I so resistant to reflecting on this text more carefully?" After reading a passage of the Bible, we shouldn't be surprised if it begins to read us.

Many contemporary aids to lectio divina include these types of questions for reflection to help the readers enter into the process of meditatio. Because lectio divina is a prayerful experience involving the whole person, these questions should respond to all levels of the personality: the intellectual, the affective, and the behavioral—the head, the heart, and the hands.

The Diverse Senses of Scripture

When we consider the many ways that Scripture can speak to us personally, it may be helpful to reflect on the patristic writers' understanding that biblical passages contain not just a literal sense, but different spiritual senses as well. If we open ourselves to these spiritual senses, we can go beyond the objective meaning of the text and experience God's word in a more profound way.

The literal sense, as we have seen, is the original meaning of a passage, the sense of the text intended by its author. This literal sense, always the foundational meaning of a text, gives rise to three spiritual senses: allegorical, moral, and anagogical.

The allegorical sense points us to Christ and his paschal mystery, through persons, events, and language in the text that represent his saving work. The moral sense of a text teaches us what Scripture has to say about discipleship and how we ought to live as Christians. The anagogical sense points to our eternal destiny and our desire for union with God—"anagogical" actually derives from *anagein*, an ancient Greek word meaning "lift up." Reflecting on these spiritual senses can help us to make vital connections between the Old and New Testaments and between the Scriptures and our spiritual lives today.

When we are mindful of both the literal and spiritual senses in our meditation, the biblical narratives become much more than stories from the ancient past. The Passover, for example, was the central event in Israel's formative history, but also has a powerful connection to our Christian life. As many spiritual writers have shown, it is fulfilled in Christ's cross and resurrection (allegorical sense). Reading about how God delivered the Israelites from slavery helps us understand how to live Christ's paschal mystery more fully in the midst of life's trials and temptations (moral sense).

The Passover, finally, can give us glimpses of the ultimate freedom and abundant life God wishes to give us through Christ's redemption (anagogical sense). The story points to the fact that the same God who liberated his people from the bondage of Egypt continues to work in similar ways with us today.

A medieval verse summarizes the literal and spiritual senses of Scripture:

> The meaning of the letter tells us about events;
> Allegory teaches what we should believe;
> The moral meaning about what we should do;
> The anagogical about what we should strive for.[3]

The allegorical sense draws meanings from the text that reinforce our faith. The moral sense extracts teachings that strengthen our charity; the anagogical brings out those elements that fortify our hope. Just as God did not create the world all at once, but continually creates, so the Spirit continuously creates meaning in the Scriptures. He continues to write the story of salvation on the pages of our very lives, as we become conformed to the gospel.

As we meditate on the pages of Scripture, we can consider the three spiritual senses by asking ourselves three questions: "How does the text relate to Jesus?" "How does it relate to me?" "How does it relate to the future?" Our lives in Christ, today and tomorrow, are the heart of God's word, and this realization goes a long way in helping us answer the question, "What does this text say to me?"

Meditating with the Imagination

In the *Spiritual Exercises*, St. Ignatius (sixteenth century) teaches readers how to use the imaginative faculty in order to make Scriptural meditation come alive. He instructs us to enter into the scene of the text with our imaginations. We are to consider the five bodily senses: What might we see? What sounds would we hear? We try to imagine the feel of the environment, the smells and tastes we would experience in the scene.

We might identify with someone in the scene and imagine what it would be like to be that person. Or we might picture ourselves there, watching and listening to what is going on. Then we are to go beneath the senses to our minds and hearts. "What am I thinking and feeling at this moment?" If it is a gospel scene, "what is it like to look into the eyes of Jesus and to know his presence? What is he telling me? How do I respond?"

Meditatio in the Life of Mary

Mary is the model of meditatio. Not only did she listen profoundly to God's word, but she reflected on that divine word throughout her life. Luke's gospel demonstrates this dimension of Mary's life most profoundly. He writes, "Mary treasured all these words and pondered them in her heart" (Luke 2:19). This treasuring of God's word, pondering it in the heart, is the essence of meditatio.

All those who want to be disciples of Jesus must likewise ponder the Scriptures in their hearts. To "ponder" suggests that the word has enough weight and gravity to shape and expand the understanding of the heart. The word of God can form our hearts when we allow it to rest within us and gradually mold our thoughts, desires, insights, judgments, and yearnings.

Later in Luke's gospel, when Mary and the brothers of Jesus approached him, Jesus said, "My mother and my brothers are those who hear the word of God and do it" (Luke 8:21). This scene forms the ideal conclusion of the parable of the sower, which teaches about the different attitudes we can take to God's word (8:1-15). In contrast to those who let the word fade away in time of testing, and those who become strangled by the distractions of worldly existence, those who protect the word and nurture it within themselves are the faithful family of Jesus. Certainly Luke affirms that Mary is not only in the family of Jesus, but a faithful disciple, a model for those who hear the word of God and keep it.

None received the word more fully and faithfully than Mary. She heard the word, kept it, and pondered it in her heart. She always preserved an attitude of attentive listening, allowing the word to rest within her, to form her mind, and stir her heart.

Questions for Reflection or Discussion

1. What is the purpose of meditatio? What might be some ways of linking the ancient biblical texts with your life today?

2. Why is the hidden truth or interior understanding of scriptural texts not always obvious? How does meditatio search for this personal meaning?

3. Why is meditatio described as a "chewing" or "ruminating" on the word? Why is this type of meditation so necessary to digest and be nourished by the food of Scripture?

4. In what ways can asking questions of the biblical text create an effective and personal meditatio? Have you had the experience of being asked questions by the text?

5. How can a search for the spiritual senses of a scriptural passage enrich our response to God's word? What are the connections they form between the ancient text and our lives today?

6. Think of an example of how you might meditate on a biblical text through the use of your imagination.

Chapter Five

Oratio: Praying in Response to God's Word

W hile lectio asks the question, "What does this text say?" and meditatio asks, "What does this text say to me?" oratio raises the question, "What do I want to say to God after reading and reflecting on this text?" After we have listened to and meditated on a biblical passage in an increasingly personal way, we naturally want to respond. Since it is ultimately God who speaks to us through the *sacra pagina*, we address our prayerful reply to the One whose voice we have heard.

One of the essential characteristics of lectio divina is its conversational nature. It is fundamentally a dialogue with God. In lectio and meditatio we listen to God; in oratio we speak to God. Lectio divina is essentially a gentle alternation between listening to God and responding to him in prayer. The two movements complement each other: reflective listening leads spontaneously to prayer.

Moving from *Lectio* and *Meditatio* to Prayer from the Heart

As the movements of lectio and meditatio grow stronger within us, we seek to read the text more in terms of our own questions, challenges, and experiences. As we listen in a way that becomes increasingly more personal, we realize that God is speaking to us and offering us a message that is unique to our own lives. The moment eventually arrives when we must ask ourselves, "Now how am I going to respond to God?" Once we realize God's call to us, his personal challenge, or the insight he is trying to give us, we must answer. We need to ask ourselves, "Will I accept or not? Will I change or not? Will I leave my comfortable satisfaction and respond to the living God?" This is the moment for prayer.

To call oratio the "moment of prayer" does not mean that our reading and meditation are not also forms of prayer. Prayer is not suddenly born in this third movement of lectio divina. All of lectio divina makes up the listening and responding that is the dialogue of prayer. Prayer accompanies us as we read the inspired page and ponder its meaning. Yet, there is a special moment within this conversation with God that we can specifically consecrate to prayer from the heart. This is oratio.

Our response to God in oratio is not just any form of prayer. In the context of lectio divina, oratio is rooted directly in prayerful reading and meditation on the scriptural text. The words that we attentively listened to in lectio and reflected on in meditatio then become the words of our prayer. The biblical words are not only at the center of our listening, they are also the heart of our response.

Depending on what we hear God saying to us in our lectio and meditatio, our prayer may be an act of praise or thanksgiving, of petition or repentance. In some cases, our prayer may even be a rebellion, a crying lament, or an angry tirade, as we see in the literature of Job, Jeremiah, and some of the psalms. The key to oratio is that our prayerful response to God flows directly from our listening.

As we listen and reflect on God's word, we must be willing to stop when we find ourselves turning to God in prayer. Stopping can be difficult for those who discover they are addicted to reading. They have their own agenda for how much they intend to read, and they refuse to stop to enter the movement of oratio. Lectio divina must be a genuine dialogue with God—a listening and a response.

St. Teresa of Avila (sixteenth century) provides us with a helpful analogy to aid us in striking the proper balance between reading and prayer, and in nurturing the gift of oratio. She explains that when a small fire has been lighted by our prayers, we may need to place a twig or two on the fire from time to time—such as a few words of Scripture—in order to keep it burning. However, she cautions that we should not throw branches upon it—meaning lengthy reading of Scripture and mental activity—because this will extinguish the flame.[1]

In lectio divina, our prayer goes hand in hand with reading and meditation. These movements do not mechanically shift from one to another. Rather, each movement forms around a spiral in which we continually travel through reading, meditation, and prayer, but each time on a new level. Through this spiral motion, we move upward toward a greater awareness of God and downward into our hearts.

Lectio Divina Teaches Us How to Pray

Sometimes we notice that our personal prayer can become rather routine and repetitive. Even when we are praying spontaneously in our own words, we often tend to repeat the same kind of prayer again and again. This is where lectio divina can be a great help in enriching our prayer.

When we practice oratio, the words of the Scriptures begin to enter our prayer language. The style and vocabulary of our personal prayers are strengthened by the inspired words of our long biblical tradition. Our prayers no longer consist of mechanically repeated formulas, but they resonate with the faith, hope, and love that animated the people of the Bible in their journey with God.

However, oratio is not meant to be just a simple repetition of the biblical text. Because of our meditation, the text has come alive for us. Because we have encountered the living God there, he has transformed our hearts. For this reason, our prayer should become a healthy combination of God's word and the words he inspires us to say. The rich deposit God leaves within us after we have meditated on his word should nourish our prayer, so that it becomes a heartfelt and Spirit-led response to him.

Oratio is an essential part of lectio divina, and we should try not to omit it. But since prayer is such an intimately personal practice, many people find it difficult to pray spontaneously, either aloud or even silently. That is why it is often helpful to spend some time writing out a personal prayer in response to our reading and meditation. We can express our feelings and desires to God in words, but we don't have to rack our brains to create excessively refined sentiments. Simplicity is the key.

The prayers of the liturgy can offer us a helpful model for forming our own prayers. If we follow the traditional elements of the Collect—invocation, petition, and conclusion—we can create our own prayers that arise directly from the Scriptures. Follow this guide as a general outline:

1. Invocation to God
2. Theme from the biblical text (past)
3. Petition drawn from the text (present)
4. Development of the petition (future)
5. Conclusion

For example, after reading and reflecting on Israel's Passover, we might form the following prayer:

God of our ancestors,
When your people cried out to you in bondage, you listened
    to their plea.
Hear my plea to you today in my distress, and free me from
    the worries that imprison my heart.
Help me to always trust in your care and to respond to the
    neglected ones around me.
I ask this in the name of Jesus and in the power of the
    Holy Spirit.

Of course, our oratio does not necessarily need to be in this form or in any other form. The more we practice this type of prayer, the more natural and heartfelt our response to God will become. All we need to do is react in the presence of the sacred text with free and spontaneous prayer.

The element we should focus on the most in this prayer is our combination of the words, images, and sentiments of the biblical text with the thoughts, needs, and desires arising within us. When our prayer remains close to the inspired page, we know that we are responding in a way that goes directly to the heart of

God. When we disregard the sacred text, our prayer may become excessively private, egotistical, or eccentric.

Language allows us to communicate, to share ourselves with God and other people. It creates relationships and brings people together. That is why in oratio, the first stage of our prayerful response to God's word, we use the vehicle of language to respond to him. Of course, God does not need us to address him in human language and with a particular vocabulary. He hears us in our hearts before we ever put anything into words. But we need words to express ourselves, and he has given us the language of Scripture to communicate with us. God uses language for our sake, to help us enter into the kind of intimacy he desires with us.

The Gift of God's Spirit Released in Our Hearts

Oratio is not only our own response to God, but it is also a gift of God. Left to ourselves, without God's grace, we would not be able to pray at all. As sinful human beings, we carry within ourselves a desire to hide from God and a reluctance to pray. Any tendency we have to avoid intimacy with God results from our fallen nature. He did not create us to live that way, and he wants to have a deeply personal relationship with each one of us.

God loves us and always takes the initiative in forming a bond with us. He uses the Scriptures to help us see ourselves as he sees us and to tell us of his loving care for us. He invites us into a dialogue with himself, a listening and responding, as between intimate friends.

In the Sermon on the Mount, Jesus urged his disciples to pray in the private recesses of their homes: "Whenever you pray, go into your room and shut the door and pray to your Father who is in secret" (Matthew 6:6). Ancient commentators understood this "inner room" as an image of the human heart, our center and our most personal dwelling. This secret place that God alone can see is the most fruitful place for prayer.

When we allow them to speak to us, the inspired Scriptures have great power to heal us from our shame and self-absorption. As we respond to God's word in prayer, we realize that it has penetrated our heart—the place where our truest self lies—and there his word has become our own word. We can now talk to God as to a dear friend, and we can relate to him as a renewed man or woman who has become a "new creation" in Christ (2 Corinthians 5:17).

When we discover an ability and desire to pray within our hearts, we know it is a gift of the Holy Spirit. Paul's letter to the Romans speaks to the uncertainty we have about our ability to pray and our fearfulness about praying well:

Likewise the Spirit helps us in our weakness; for we do not know how to pray as we ought, but that very Spirit intercedes with sighs too deep for words. And God, who searches the heart, knows what is the mind of the Spirit, because the Spirit intercedes for the saints according to the will of God. (Romans 8:26-27)

We all know our weaknesses when it comes to prayer. Our false self-sufficiency and need for control can stifle the life of grace and the gifts of the Holy Spirit within us. But if we let him take control, God promises us that his divine Spirit will come into our hearts to pray within us. Since God alone can see our hearts, he receives our Spirit-guided prayer and gives us all that we need according to his loving plan for us.

The essence of prayer is desire. St. Augustine (fifth century) expressed the great longing of the human heart for God: "You have made us for yourself, and our heart is restless until it rests in you."[2] We lose our desire for prayer when we lose the sense that we are not made for ourselves, but for God, and that only God satisfies the deepest hunger of our hearts.

Oratio is our active effort to keep our hearts open to God's Spirit by preparing the way for his work within us. Our desire is all important. In fact, Augustine said, "The desire to pray is itself prayer."[3] We discover the gift of prayer when we recover our desire for God. In oratio we eventually realize that our desire for God is itself the presence of his Spirit working within us.

The Treasury of Prayer in the Bible

The Bible is filled with prayers of various forms and styles. Though any passage of Scripture can move us to the moment of oratio, the prayers of Scripture may particularly influence the language, vocabulary, and spirit of our prayer. By offering us models for our own prayer, they are particularly helpful texts for nourishing the prayer of lectio divina.

All of the major figures of the Hebrew Scriptures offer us models of prayer. Moses was known as one who could speak face to face with God. In prayer, he was both an intercessor for the people and a partner with God in his saving work. Deborah prayed to God after her victory, and Hannah prayed for the gift of a child, then in gratitude for God's gift. The prayers of David are prayers of praise and petition, lament and contrition. Solomon prayed at the dedication of the temple for wisdom and for blessings upon God's people.

We can find the prayers of God's prophets throughout the prophetic literature. Elijah offered prayers of petition for divine favor. Jeremiah prayed his laments and complaints with unrestrained emotion. Daniel was faithful in prayer even under the most difficult of circumstances.

In Israel, prayer was not limited to prophets, kings, and priests. Prayer was practiced daily by all God's people, and it could be recited anywhere and at any time. It was both public and private, formal and personal, liturgical and spontaneous. Though biblical prayers were sometimes long and extravagant, most were short, simple, and direct. People prayed while standing, kneeling, lying prostrate on the ground, bowing, or lifting their hands. Their physical position suggested the involvement of the whole person—mind, body, emotions, and will—but what it reflected most was the attitude of the heart in relationship to God.

More significant, the people of Israel rejected the notion that prayer was magical or an attempt to manipulate God. They did not seek to flatter him or grovel for his response, but they trusted that he heard their prayer and could change their condition. They saw prayer as communication with God, a natural human response to God's self-revelation. It was an exchange of confidence between God and his people, marked by intimacy and trust.

The Book of Psalms is the only biblical work that consists entirely of prayers. We can find every type of prayer there: prayers of praise, thanksgiving, lament, petition, confidence, confession, and more. The psalmists praised God for his great glory, reflected in the wonders of the natural world, his great deeds among the people, and the joys of human life. They expressed delight in moments of blessing, and they lamented in times of loss, grief, and frustration. They brought the full range of human emotion to prayer: from confidence, happiness, and gratitude to sorrow, fear, and despair, even anger and rage. This unreserved, full-hearted prayer was Israel's way of affirming God's presence with them and being assured of his unfailing concern.

The Prayer That Jesus Taught Us

Jesus recited the psalms regularly in prayer, both in the liturgical prayer of his people and in his own personal prayer. The psalms are quoted throughout the gospels, both on the lips of Jesus and in reference to his life. Clearly, Jesus had internalized the psalms as his own prayer, and they arose spontaneously from his lips in times of joy and sorrow.

The church never composed its own book of psalms but used Israel's "prayer book" as its own. Just as the Jewish people used the psalms to pray in situations far different from those in which they were composed, the early Christians used them to express praise, thanksgiving, confidence, and lamentation. Because the psalms were the prayers of Jesus, his followers have prayed them for centuries in his name.

Through these ancient prayers, Jesus teaches us that we can pray with words that are not our own. Reciting words written thousands of years ago, we open our hearts to pray the inspired words of our ancestors. When we are praying a psalm, our feelings don't even need to be in harmony with the emotions it expresses. We open ourselves to encompass the entire body of Christ—praising, thanking, repenting, and lamenting with all of God's people. The psalms give us an opportunity to put their experiences of happiness, gratitude, grief, and anguish into our hearts and transform them into prayer. We learn to "rejoice with those who rejoice, weep with those who weep" (Romans 12:15). This anointed collection of prayers endures because of the variety of thoughts and feelings we find there and because the Holy Spirit constantly breathes life into them. After three millennia, they are still the prayers of the people of God.

Jesus taught his followers to pray by his example. The gospels show him habitually in prayer, often going away to pray in solitude. He sought communion with the Father to renew his ministry and to find direction at critical moments. We see Jesus in prayer from the beginnings of his public life until his prayer in the Garden of Gethsemane and his final prayer on the cross.

Even though the disciples prayed the psalms and the other prayers of the Jewish tradition with Jesus, they must have seen something different about the way that he prayed—something they wanted to share. So after Jesus had finished praying in a certain place, "one of his disciples said to him, 'Lord, teach us to pray'" (Luke 11:1). It was on this occasion that Jesus taught them what we know as the Lord's Prayer.

The most distinctive characteristic of Jesus' prayer is that he addressed God as "Father." Because the God of Abraham, Isaac, and Jacob was his father, Jesus addressed him with the same familiarity and affection that a son or daughter has with his or her parents. When his disciples asked Jesus to teach them to pray, they were asking to enter into this intimate relationship with the Father. So Jesus taught them to turn to his father as their father, to pray to God as "our Father." Jesus taught them to pray in this way because he was establishing a new relationship between God and his disciples, making them sons and daughters of God.

Through Jesus' saving death and resurrection and the presence of his Spirit within us, we are adopted as children of God, and we can address him as "Abba," Father. And so our prayers, like the Lord's Prayer, can be simple and confident. Prayers worthy of God's attention do not have to be wordy or elaborate. A child can simply ask for basic needs on a daily basis, as well as express gratitude for the good things a parent provides. There is no need to multiply words or create formal, artificial language. Our God knows our hearts and our needs. We can pray to him with assurance and trust.

The Lord's Prayer is inspired Scripture, and we can pray it without hesitation because it comes directly from the heart of Jesus. But it is also a model for all of our oratio. Whenever we pray, we can use words that are natural for us, that reveal what is really in our minds and hearts. We can freely express our praise of God when we worship, our sorrow when we are sad, our joy when we are happy, and our apology when we are repentant. Simplicity, directness, honesty, and confidence—these are the qualities of prayer that Jesus teaches us and the marks that characterize the oratio of a disciple.

Oratio in the Life of Mary

Because Mary had spent her whole life listening to the word of God, she could listen attentively to the new words spoken by the angel Gabriel at the annunciation. Because she had learned to meditate on God's word in her youth, she was able to reflect on what the angelic word of God meant to her. And finally, after her lectio and meditatio, she was able to respond in oratio with her whole heart: "Here am I, the servant of the Lord; let it be with me according to your word" (Luke 1:38).

Mary's attitude of attentive listening had opened her heart completely and made her totally receptive to God's will. She responded to his word with simplicity, directness, honesty, and confidence. Elizabeth said of her, "Blessed is she who believed that there would be a fulfillment of what was spoken to her by the Lord" (Luke 1:45). We can model our response to God's word on that of Mary, who said, "Let it be," with simple trust.

During her visit to Elizabeth, Mary continued to reflect on the Lord's words to her. She responded to him again in her prayer of praise and thanksgiving (Luke 1:46-55). The remarkable characteristic of her Magnificat is the way that she wove verses from the psalms, the prayer of Hannah (1 Samuel 2), and other Old Testament prayers into her own prayer. Mary had obviously learned these traditional prayers as a young girl, as she heard the Hebrew Scriptures recited constantly. Words from these texts spontaneously rose from her heart to her lips. But she did not simply repeat the prayers of her ancestors; she prayed a completely new prayer that embodied both those ancient texts and the divine word she had heard. Allowing God's word to interact with her own thoughts, feelings, memories, hopes, and desires, she responded in a beautiful biblical prayer that came from the depths of her heart.

Questions for Reflection or Discussion

1. If all of lectio divina is prayer, what is the particular quality of oratio? In what sense is oratio a response to God?

2. In what way can lectio divina enrich your prayer to God? In what sense is oratio a combination of the vocabulary of Scripture and the thoughts, needs, and desires that arise from your heart?

3. Why is prayer a gift from God's Spirit? How can you receive and activate the gift of prayer within yourself?

4. What is most notable to you about the quality of the prayers found throughout the Bible?

5. What did Jesus teach his disciples about prayer when they asked him to teach them to pray? What characteristics of the Lord's Prayer do you want to incorporate into your own prayer?

6. In what ways do the prayers of Mary serve as a model for the prayer of oratio?

Chapter Six

Contemplatio: Quietly Resting in God

All the movements of lectio divina we have discussed thus far have involved the use of words. In lectio we carefully read the words of Scripture. In meditatio we reflect on the implications of those inspired words for our own lives. In oratio we respond to God's word with words of our own in prayer. But eventually words become unnecessary; they have taken us as far as they can. The movement of contemplatio is mostly wordless silence. We quietly rest in the presence of God. We simply accept and receive the transforming embrace of the One who has led us to this moment.

Moving from Active Prayer to Contemplative Prayer

The movements of lectio divina are more like the colors of a rainbow than clearly defined stages. They often overlap, blending into one another, ebbing and flowing according to the rhythm of the divine Spirit and the human heart. Oratio is the path that leads to contemplatio, but the moment when active prayer moves to contemplative prayer is often unclear.

Both oratio and contemplatio are prayer that arises from the heart. Oratio is word-filled prayer: our words in response to God's word. Contemplatio is prayer with few words. It is the response to God that remains after words are no longer necessary or helpful. In contemplatio we no longer have to think or reason, listen or speak. We experience moments of this kind of wordless presence in any loving relationship. Contemplatio is simply enjoying the experience of quietly being in God's presence. Though we might think the movement of contemplatio is passive and uneventful, it is not. God's grace is truly at work there, and his Holy Spirit is changing us without our direct knowledge.

Resistance to *Contemplatio* Today

Around the sixteenth century, theologians began to separate contemplation from what they considered the normal experience of prayer for most Christians. They placed contemplation in its own category as a type of mystical experience that was reserved only for rare individuals. Until recent decades, spiritual writers defined it as a higher form of union with God, one that most people could never reach. Unfortunately, this reserved attitude about contemplation remains in the popular mind today and often discourages people from learning how to move into this kind of prayer.

In earlier centuries, however, the church did not consider contemplation as an exclusive form of prayer. Theologians understood it as a higher stage, reached along the road of receptive listening and vocal prayer, but believed it was a natural phase of prayer available to anyone with an open heart.

Today there are other forms of resistance to contemplation as a result of the mind-set of our culture. In Western society, we define people primarily by their *doing* rather than their *being*. We judge our own life and that of others by our successes and achievements. According to this way of thinking, simply being in the presence of God without accomplishing anything seems like a waste of time to many people.

This Western mind-set is contrary to the direction of contemplation. Our lack of appreciation for "being" and our overvalued emphasis on "doing" creates a void in our society that explains our great attraction toward Eastern spirituality. People are searching for a greater spiritual depth than our culture offers us. We want a way of relating to the "Higher Power" that does not depend on what we do and what we accomplish, but on who we are at the deepest level. This is the kind of mindfulness and awareness of the divine that contemplatio can give us.

All of the material and technological accomplishments of the twenty-first century are not without their price. Never before in history have societies been so prone to analyze, intellectualize, and control everything about people's lives. Today the analytical faculties of our minds tend to overpower the intuitive faculties that we need so much for contemplation. Our pragmatic intellects have triumphed over the receptive intuition that brings us into communion with the divine.

Because contemplatio demands that we let go of any effort to be "in charge" of our lives, it is more difficult for us to practice today than in previous ages. Because of our modern attitude, the development of contemplatio seems much less spontaneous and natural now than it was in earlier centuries. For this reason—even though our hearts are naturally attracted to union with God—we often exclude contemplatio from our prayers.

A final reason we resist contemplatio is our tendency to misrepresent contemplative people as dreamy and withdrawn from the world. In stories about saints and mystics, contemplation has often been associated with unusual phenomena detached from ordinary life. But these caricatures prevent us from realizing how many authentically contemplative people live among us. Contrary to this distorted picture, genuine contemplation promotes what is most authentically human within us. In fact, it can be argued that contemplative union with God is the most human experience that life offers.

Contemplation does not separate us from other people; rather, it helps us experience a truer union with humanity than the superficial connections our culture offers today. Contemplation does not make us less concerned for the world in which we live, but more concerned. The Trappist monk Thomas Merton (twentieth century) said that contemplation is out of the question for anyone who doesn't try to cultivate compassion for others. Contemplation and compassion both lead us to a fuller expression of our humanity.

Nurturing the Interior Life of Contemplation

Lectio divina progresses as we move from realizing God's presence in his word to being aware of his presence within us. Thomas Keating (twentieth and twenty-first centuries) describes this progression: "The external word of God in Scripture awakens us to the interior Word of God in our inmost being."[1] It is a movement from conversation to communion.

However, we can never force this transition from oratio to contemplatio. It is always a matter of our receptivity to God's grace. Our task is to remove as many obstacles to his Spirit as we can: our inner resistance, our awareness of time, our desire to control the process, and our self-concern. We must remain lovingly attentive to God and experience the desire for interior silence. When we feel God drawing us into a deeper awareness of his divine presence, we gradually abandon our intellectual activity and let ourselves be wooed into his embrace. The experience resembles that of lovers holding each other in wordless silence or of a sleeping child resting in the arms of its mother.

The most practical thing we can do to cultivate an interior atmosphere for contemplatio is to create spaces in our life each day for silence. But the volume of noise that fills our environment keeps growing. The ceaseless clatter bombarding us from media entertainment, cell phones, digital devices, and other sources is very difficult to extinguish. Because this noise is such a constant part of life, some people cannot handle silence. We sometimes even fear it, as children fear the dark. Because we are so used to external stimulation, we are afraid that silence may bring up thoughts from deep inside ourselves. We dread these inner thoughts that might reveal something we don't want to hear—so we pump up the volume around us to keep the thoughts at bay.

In contrast to the rapid, noisy communication that technology makes possible, quiet, receptive stillness is the atmosphere in which the most important communication occurs. If we spend all of our time in extroverted activity, we become strangers to our own inner life. By denying ourselves the environment in which to cultivate contemplation, we deny ourselves a fuller understanding of our true self and the personal transformation made possible through a deeper relationship with God.

The Practice of *Contemplatio*

Of all the movements of lectio divina, contemplatio is the most difficult to describe because it is such a personal moment with

God. It is also the moment that we most often omit from our practice because of the types of resistance discussed above.

But if we can get past our contemporary struggles with silence and intimacy with God, we will find that contemplation is one of the most satisfying and enriching experiences we can have.

Thomas Aquinas (thirteenth century) said that contemplatio puts us in touch with God so that our soul can rest in joy and repose, because it possesses the One it loves. Though we often fear this level of intimacy, it is a natural experience for those in a deepening relationship with God. Contemplatio is a type of prayer that is available to all, and it is a normal part of the serious Christian life.

We must never pass over contemplatio in our practice of lectio divina. In fact, one could argue that contemplatio is the most essential element in lectio divina, even though it seems the most "useless" from a practical point of view. After listening to the Scriptures, reflecting on them, and responding to God through active prayer, we must always then enter into silence. This quiet resting in God does not need to be a prolonged period, though the more we practice lectio divina, the more we will begin to relish this period of silence.

Remember that contemplatio is all about receptivity; it is God's gift that we can only receive with gratitude. It can never be a planned process. Contemplatio is our attempt to stand before God with no pretensions. In contemplatio, the heart—the center of our being, and the place where we are most truly ourselves— is humbly exposed to him. What happens within us during these moments is really not up to us. Contemplatio slowly works at transforming our hearts, offering us a taste of the divine life we are destined to share.

The center of Christian contemplation is Christ himself. It is a heart-to-heart encounter. Our own heart—the place where our thoughts, desires, memories, and affections meet—is placed in the Sacred Heart of Jesus. In that encounter we are in touch with God and in touch with ourselves at a deep level. Though there is often no sign of God at work in our silence, his invisible and unknowable presence is working within us because we have opened our life to Christ.

Touching the Life of the Trinity

There are lots of good and practical reasons to read and pray the Bible, but the truest function of God's revelation and all Christian prayer is to lead us to a deeper sharing in the very life of God. In his letter to the Christians in Ephesus, Paul described this sharing as being "filled with all the fullness of God." He spoke of the profound mystery of our relationship with the Father, Son, and Holy Spirit:

> [14]I bow my knees before the Father, [15]from whom every family in heaven and on earth takes its name. [16]I pray that, according to the riches of his glory, he may grant that you may be strengthened in your inner being with power through his Spirit, [17]and that Christ may dwell in your hearts through faith, as you are being rooted and grounded in love. [18]I pray that you may have the power to comprehend, with all the saints, what is the breadth and length and height and depth, [19]and to know the love of Christ that

surpasses knowledge, so that you may be filled with all the fullness of God. [20]Now to him who by the power at work within us is able to accomplish abundantly far more than all we can ask or imagine, [21]to him be glory in the church and in Christ Jesus to all generations, forever and ever. Amen. (Ephesians 3:14-21)

We kneel in adoration and prayer before God the Father, who is the creator of every community in heaven and on earth. Out of the glorious riches of God, the Holy Spirit imparts power to strengthen us from within. Through our response to God in faith, Christ takes up residence in our hearts, dwelling in our innermost being.

As the Holy Spirit renews us and as Christ lives within us, we are being "rooted and grounded in love." The ability to comprehend "the breadth and length and height and depth" of God's life depends on love. Growing in God's life is not just a matter of increasing knowledge and understanding; it is the contemplative process of deepening our union with God in love.

Through our receptivity to God, not through our own efforts, he works within us and "is able to accomplish abundantly far more than all we can ask or imagine." Contemplatio takes us beyond words, beyond knowledge, where God takes the initiative in transforming us in his love. When we open our lives for him to work deep within us, we allow him to do more to change us from within than we could ever hope for. The same divine treasury of love that suffuses the vastness of creation also penetrates the boundless depths of our hearts.

In the divine Trinity, love forever flows between the Father and the Son in the Holy Spirit. Prayer is already going on in the heart of God. In lectio divina, we do not just establish a conversation with God, but we enter a relationship that is already in full swing between the Father, Son, and Spirit. In contemplatio we are invited to participate in the intimacy of the Trinity.

Contemplatio in the Life of Mary

Mary nurtured a contemplative experience of God through her relationship to the Word of God, from her own nurturing womb to his rock-hewn tomb. After Christ's resurrection and ascension, Mary waited with the other disciples for God to send the Holy Spirit (Acts 1:14). This expectant waiting for the transforming work of the Spirit is the model for the contemplative life.

Through her relationship with the earthly and the glorified Christ, Mary shows us the prayerful union that leads to contemplation. Cultivating her prayer through an active relationship to her Son throughout his life, Mary prepared for the receptive waiting of contemplative prayer. Simply resting in trustful confidence that God would send the Spirit with his multiple gifts and transforming power, Mary demonstrated for us how to transition to the prayer of contemplatio.

In Mary's outward form, in what our eyes and ears perceive, she is the humble servant of the Lord. But in her inward form, she is the fullness of grace. As beloved daughter of the Father, tender mother of the Son, and loving spouse of the Holy Spirit, she reveals that she is rooted entirely in the Trinity.

Christian theology describes Mary as the *Theotokos*—the bearer of God. Holding her Son in her womb and in her heart,

Mary gave birth to him in the world. As the icon of Christian contemplation, Mary invites us to participate in her own wondrous gaze at this divine gift, and then to bring forth the Word into the world today.

Questions for Reflection or Discussion

1. What are some of the main differences between the prayer of oratio and the prayer of contemplatio?

2. What kinds of resistance do you sense within yourself to the prayer of contemplatio?

3. What can you do to cultivate the gift of contemplation in your own daily life?

4. In what sense is contemplatio a heart-to-heart encounter with God? Why is it the most essential element of lectio divina, even though it seems the most "useless"?

5. In what way do the words of Ephesians 3:14-21 speak personally to you about the experience of prayer?

6. In what way is Mary the ideal image of Christian contemplation? What can you learn from her about the contemplative life?

Chapter Seven

Operatio: Faithful Witness in Daily Life

In the parable of the sower, Jesus gave us this metaphor: "The seed is the word of God" (Luke 8:11). If we begin with this organic image, we can expand it to the movements of lectio divina. Lectio is the sprouting of the plant, and meditatio is the leafing. In a healthy plant, oratio and contemplatio are surely the budding and the blossoming. Extending this metaphor through the cycle of life, operatio is the delicate fruit that gradually ripens on the hearty plant of sacred reading. The fertile blossom and the ripened fruit, of course, bring forth new seeds for the growth of new plants, as the cycle of prayerful reading continues.

Operatio is our lived response to the scriptural text. After reading, reflecting, and praying over the word, we should be impacted in a way that makes a difference in our daily life. The question operatio asks of us is, "How can I live out the word of God which I have heard in my heart?"

Every biblical text has a call or challenge to those who listen to its sacred words. We cannot prayerfully read Scripture without being changed in some specific way. Our sacred reading must have an effect beyond the prayerful exercise itself. Through lectio divina we evangelize ourselves. We build bridges between the text and daily life. In operatio we become witnesses of God's kingdom and members of the body of Christ in the world.

Living out the word of God that we have heard in our hearts can be as simple as helping a person in need or being kind to someone we don't like. It can be as demanding as the call to reconcile with someone who is estranged from us or as an urgency to change some aspect of our career. But operatio always arises from prayerfully encountering God as we listen to Scripture.

The Unity of Contemplatio and Operatio

The word of God draws us inward to that deep place within ourselves where we find God; it also impels us outward to those places in need of the light of the divine word. Contemplatio and operatio are not two separate and distinct movements. Their impulses grow together in the heart of one who prayerfully reads Scripture. Contemplatio does not separate us from the world, and operatio is not genuine unless it grows out of contemplative reflection. Compassion arises from contemplation, and the call of operatio arises out of a compassionate heart. We do not have one heart for God and another for human beings.

Contemplatio enables us to realize that God is not absent from life's daily reality. If we are blind to God's presence in the world of our family and our work, in political action and issues of justice, contemplatio opens our eyes. Contemplation is seeing the deepest meaning of issues, problems, and events. Through contemplatio we savor the creative presence of God's word, and thereby open ourselves to become more deeply involved in the transformational process that the word has provoked throughout human history.

Apart from contemplatio, operatio becomes superficial pragmatism. We must never view the Bible as simply a collection of maxims to be put into practice. Rather, operatio must always flow from the prayerful process of lectio divina. Embracing the word through listening and prayer, we allow it to become the source of the active response we make in daily life.

The practical proposals and working projects that we conceive in operatio may often seem very general. Rarely does Scripture offer us concrete details about what to do in specific situations. The word of God helps us to plumb the depths of issues and teaches us what is essential. Out of this wisdom, we can choose a number of possible courses of action. Our human reason and experience must always accompany our prayerful discernment as we decide how to live out the word of God

We cannot separate contemplatio and operatio from one another if their results are to be a genuine work of God's Spirit. Throughout history, many of Christianity's most ardent activists have also been the most fervent contemplatives. Sacred reading helps us to be contemplative activists and active contemplatives. In other words, lectio divina helps us to become saints.

The Fruitfulness of God's Word

A person's word is weighed not only by the ideas it communicates, but by the results it achieves. If a person does what they promise to do, their word has integrity. The saying "You're only as good as your word" illustrates the bond between a person's effectiveness and the words they express.

God's word not only communicates ideas but contains the power to create change. As the psalmist sings, "By the word of the LORD the heavens were made" (Psalm 33:6). That divine word continues to create and is the primary cause of the world's ongoing existence.

So many of the words that we speak and hear throughout the day have no effect. But the word that goes forth from the "mouth" of God always achieves its purpose. In a beautiful poetic metaphor, the prophet Isaiah speaks about God's word as a penetrating rain and blanketing snow, giving moisture to the earth so that it may bear fruit:

> For as the rain and the snow come down from heaven,
> and do not return there until they have watered
> the earth,
> making it bring forth and sprout,
> giving seed to the sower and bread to the eater,
> so shall my word be that goes out from my mouth;
> it shall not return to me empty,
> but it shall accomplish that which I purpose,
> and succeed in the thing for which I sent it.
> (Isaiah 55:10-11)

As the rain and the snow fall to the earth, they meet a yearning receptivity. The ground receives their welcome moisture as an assurance that the seeds will sprout and eventually bear fruit. Sometimes God's word falls on deaf ears or distracted minds. But if we listen and open our hearts, eventually that word will penetrate the parched soil of our lives. Not only will God's word refresh us and help us to grow, it will cause us to bear the fruit that God intends for us to share.

God desires his word to have an effect on us, but it will not unless we activate the power within it. As James wrote, "Be doers of the word, and not merely hearers" (James 1:22). Though listening is the first movement of sacred reading, putting the word into action is the culminating result. Through the process of prayerful reading, God's word will achieve its purposes within us and bring forth renewed life.

The power of God's word is not just confined to our hearts. The change it effects in us makes for change in the world. Being a "doer of the word" enables us to act as instruments of God's grace so that he may bring his loving purpose to fulfillment. Our obedience to the word planted in our hearts makes us channels for his compassion and mercy.

Formed as Disciples through the Word

To prayerfully read the Scriptures is to listen to Christ speaking to us. As Hugh of St. Victor (twelfth century) explained, "All Sacred Scripture is but one book, and this one book is Christ."[1] Lectio divina is not so much a matter of interpreting a book as of seeking Christ and learning to follow him. Reflecting on the sacred texts should become for us a joyful discovery of Christ and a devoted process of becoming his disciple.

Through lectio divina, our hearts and minds are formed in the way of Christ as we deepen our relationship with him. In this interaction of master and disciple, Christ communicates his life to us and leads us toward a growing identification with him. As we develop this personal bond with Christ, then our actions, too, become vehicles of his presence to others.

This formation takes place in gradual and progressive stages. First, we listen to Jesus and make the choice to follow him. We attach our life to his, and we lovingly study his teachings. As our discipleship progresses, we not only listen to what he says but also imitate what he does. Discipleship becomes a matter of both listening to his words and living as he lived. Christ's example becomes part of us, so that we begin to act as he acted in all the challenging circumstances of life.

As discipleship develops, the relationship of master and disciple becomes increasingly focused inward. More than externally following Christ's teachings, we start to become like him. We become his likeness for others, representing him in our own environments. In our speech and our actions we hope to be "another Christ."

Finally, at the highest stage of discipleship, we seek to be totally identified with Christ. We begin to experience Christ working within us, as we allow his Spirit to become the source of our activity. Then we come to understand the experience Paul was referring to in his address to the Galatians: "It is no longer I who live, but it is Christ who lives in me" (Galatians 2:20).

This is the goal of the Christian life—to be and live "in Christ." Lectio divina initiates us into the way of Christ and leads us from an external obedience toward an internal participation in his life. This is the life of grace that begins in our baptism and is deepened throughout our lives. Because of this spiritual identification with Christ and participation in him, our actions become more his work than our own. In contemplatio we become the subject of Christ's prayer, and in operatio Christ becomes the doer of our actions. In this mystical bond with Christ, we see the true depths of discipleship that can be created through lectio divina.

The Word Leads to Discernment and Decision Making

One of the great proponents of lectio divina in our times has been Cardinal Carlo M. Martini, SJ. In his younger years he was a professor of Scripture and then became rector of the Pontifical Biblical Institute in Rome. In later years he was the archbishop of Milan. As a teacher and pastor, Cardinal Martini responded to the request of some young people in his diocese to teach them how to pray with the Bible. He formed the School of the Word in the cathedral with three hundred present the first evening. The numbers soon grew to several thousand, overflowing the cathedral. The monthly sessions were then held in dozens of parishes throughout the diocese and broadcasted to the churches by radio.

Cardinal Martini's method of lectio combines sound interpretation of the text with a pastoral reading. By helping his listeners understand the context and literal meaning of a passage, he leads them into the process of listening personally to the word. In addition to the traditional four-step method outlined by Guigo (*lectio, meditatio, oratio,* and *contemplatio*), Martini adds additional movements taken from the monastic tradition and from the spiritual teachings of St. Ignatius of Loyola (sixteenth century). The additional elements comprising his eight steps include *consolatio, discretio, deliberatio,* and *actio.*[2] Through these four movements, Martini moves the prayerful reader from contemplation to action, tracing an outward progression from lectio divina back to daily life. It is helpful to briefly describe these four movements, which are actually distinct phases of operatio and can help us to follow the path of discipleship.

Consolatio is an experience of deep joy that arises from prayerfully reflecting on the Scriptures when we are being moved in the direction of God's will. It widens our vision, releases new energy for life, and gives us encouragement and peace. More than a good feeling, consolatio is a gift of the Holy Spirit working within us as we encounter the living Christ in prayer and contemplation.

Consolatio creates the spiritual "atmosphere" in which we can make decisions and choices that are true to our most authentic self. God's desire for each one of us is that we should be peaceful and joyful, and he has spiritually programmed us to gain consolation from doing what is right. So in the process of making a choice or choosing our life's direction, we should feel comfortable and consoled in the direction that is most in tune with God's purpose for us. If we feel enthusiasm for one choice and dryness in regard to other options, these internal emotions gradually lead us to knowledge of where our heart lies and where God is prompting us.

Discretio is the process of discernment. It provides us with a kind of spiritual radar for the way of Christ, making us sensitive to what is in line with the gospel and what is not. Sacred reading of Scripture leads us to an awareness of God's presence in our hearts, showing us things as they really are. As the light of God's word shines into the darkness of our confusion and uncertainty, we can more easily see the subtle differences between what is of God and what is not of God.

We attain this ability to discern by entering into "the mind of Christ" through our prayerful reading and reflection. This stirs up the gifts of the Holy Spirit within us: wisdom, understanding, counsel, knowledge, fortitude, piety, and fearful reverence for God (Isaiah 11:2-3). With the indwelling of the Spirit, we are able to be sensitive to the presence of God and look at life as God sees it. The gifts of the Spirit help us to make decisions and live them out, so we can follow the way of discipleship.

Paul desired this discernment for all Christ's disciples: "Be transformed by the renewing of your minds, so that you may discern what is the will of God—what is good and acceptable and perfect" (Romans 12:2). Discretio is not just doing exactly what the Bible says. Lectio divina offers us a true transformation into Christ, helping us to set our heart on the things of the Spirit. Discretio offers us the wisdom and understanding that are the Spirit's gifts.

Deliberatio is the moment of making a decision. Our decisiveness about what to do and what not to do is the result of reflection and discernment, enabling us to know what is in harmony with the Holy Spirit's guidance. Deciding what is right and good in a given situation, what we ought to do as a disciple of Jesus, takes us beyond simply following moral rules. Through deliberatio Jesus invites us to shape our lives as disciples in terms of our commitment to him.

After discretio and deliberatio comes actio, the mature fruit of the whole process. Actio is the moment in which we live what we have learned through lectio divina. Prayerful reading shapes our being and thereby shapes our action. We live out who we have become through the process of lectio divina.

Actualization of the Ancient Text

To "actualize" the Scripture means to bring it into the present. The word of God as we find it written in the Bible stands at a distance in time from our culture, from our concerns, and from our daily life. But God intends the Bible to reach all people in their concrete, present existence. So to actualize sacred Scripture means to make the meaning of his word accessible to people today.

Actualization is a relatively new term in biblical interpretation. It has come into wider usage through the Pontifical Biblical Commission's *The Interpretation of the Bible in the Church* (Vatican City, 1993). Actualization, as it is used in this document, comes from the French *actualiser*—"to bring up to date" or "to become real."

The document points out how actualization is already present within the Bible itself. Ancient texts were reread in light of new circumstances and applied to new situations in the lives of God's people. For example, the encouraging word of God given in the context of Israel's slavery in Egypt was applied centuries later to the new situation of Israel's exile. Isaiah 40–55 uses the words and images of the Book of Exodus to give hope to God's people held in the bondage of Babylon. The exodus from Babylon would repeat the exodus from Egypt in a whole new context. God would bring his people out of bondage with a flourish of divine power even greater than the deliverance from Egypt hundreds of years before.

Actualization is possible because the fullness of meaning contained in the biblical texts gives them a value for all times and all cultures. This basic conviction encourages believing communities today to continue this process of bringing the word of God into the present by expressing its relevance to new times and circumstances.

Actualization is the task of the whole church—preachers, teachers, writers, and all who practice lectio divina. According to the biblical commission, this task involves first seeking the meaning of the words in their original contexts and, after we have understood their historical meaning, finding the points that can be actualized in the life of the believer and of the Christian community. The challenge is to get beyond the historical conditioning in order to determine the essential message of the text.

The commission listed three steps in the interpretive task of actualization: 1) to hear the word from within one's own concrete situation; 2) to identify the aspects of the present situation highlighted or put into question by the text; 3) to draw from the fullness of meaning contained in the biblical text those elements capable of advancing the present situation in a way that is productive and consonant with the saving will of God in Christ.[3]

Through actualization, the Bible can shed light on many issues for the world, the church, and the lives of those who prayerfully read the text. The process of actualization works by the same principles that underlie the action of operatio—faithful witness to the word of God in daily life. With the Bible in one hand and the newspaper in the other, we can respond to the scriptural text in a way that makes a difference in the world.

Operatio in the Life of Mary

Mary's entire life was a response to the word of God, beginning with her youthful reply to the angel at the annunciation: "Let it be with me according to your word" (Luke 1:38). From Nazareth to Jerusalem, she was a faithful witness to the Word to which she had given her yes. Even in her most difficult moments standing beneath the cross of her son, Mary never retracted her commitment to live in total openness to God.

As a model for our operatio, Mary offers us words of trusting encouragement for our task of faithfully witnessing to the word. At the beginning of Jesus' public ministry in John's gospel, Mary was present at a wedding feast with Jesus and his disciples. When the wine ran out, Mary instructed the servants, "Do whatever he tells you" (John 2:5). She knew that Jesus would transform the water he found there into the vibrant wine of God's kingdom.

As mother of the disciples after the resurrection, Mary tells us to prepare to do whatever Jesus asks of us. She knows that being "a doer of the word" and responding to that word with trusting obedience is the way to our well-being and happiness. Through operatio, Jesus will take our ordinary lives and shape them into instruments for building his kingdom. Through faithful witness to the word, we will be disciples of Jesus in the world today.

Questions for Reflection or Discussion

1. Why is it so important that operatio flow from contemplatio? What happens within your own life when you do not maintain the essential unity between contemplatio and operatio?

2. In what way do the words of Isaiah 55:10-11 speak personally to you about the meaning of operatio?

3. Describe the deepening process of discipleship that is created through lectio divina. In what way have you experienced the movement from external obedience to interior union in Christ?

4. How could the additional movements of lectio divina used by Cardinal Carlo Martini help you in the path of discipleship and decision making?

5. What example can you give of actualization of a biblical text?

6. In what way are the movements of consolatio, discretio, and deliberatio exhibited in the joy and confidence of Mary's life?

Chapter Eight

Collatio: Forming Community Through Scripture

C ollatio is the communal practice of lectio divina, and its aim is to build a spiritual community around the word of God. Through conversation and shared insight, a supportive group can be an enormous help in allowing God's word to take fire in our hearts. Each individual comes to a deeper understanding of sacred Scripture by adding together the ideas and deliberations of every other person in the group.

Like the other terms associated with lectio divina, *collatio* is a Latin word, an expression which originally meant a "bringing together or comparison." In reference to speech and ideas, the term meant an "interchange or discussion." Later the word came to designate a shared meal to which everyone contributes and in which everyone partakes. For lectio divina, the shared meal is God's scriptural word.

Though the individual practice of lectio divina was the regular practice in the early centuries, there is evidence that communal lectio divina was followed in various forms in many monastic communities. Isidore of Seville (sixth century) praised the value of collatio over individual reading. He wrote, "By comparing ideas, what at first seemed obscure or doubtful becomes clear."[1]

Forming Communities of Faith, Centered on the Word

Lectio divina began in the ancient world when books were rare and precious. Because few people had their own Bibles, people would gather to hear the word read aloud, followed by a period of quiet reflection on what they had heard. They would then begin to share what each had understood from the text, which then developed into a discussion. Finally, they offered prayer to God, both aloud and in silence, in response to the word they had received.

Today this form of lectio divina is increasingly popular in developing countries where books are still hard to come by. I have personally traveled to countries in Latin America and Africa to experience this communal practice of lectio divina in a variety of contexts. It is astounding to witness the simple wisdom that arises from ordinary people when hearing, reflecting, and dialoguing over the word of God.

Christians throughout the world are forming small faith communities centered on the sacred text. This rebirth of interest in the collatio is accompanied by a deep desire among Christians to feel united to a spiritual community. This powerful movement of creating Christian community by being fashioned in God's word is having enormously transformative effects on the church in many areas of the world today.

Practical Advice and Warnings

The collatio should never take the place of regular, personal lectio divina. Rather, the communal experience should be a normal continuation of our daily sacred reading. We can often bring the insights and realizations that we have gained in our personal reflection to the group experience. The input of each participant helps the group to better appreciate and actualize the message of the sacred page.

The spirit of the collatio should be that of a personal conversation that builds up each individual in the group. Each must have a desire and willingness to learn from one another and to grow together in faith, hope, and charity. The teacher is the divine word; the members of the group are all learners.

A few warnings may help the group remain faithful to the essential purpose of the collatio. First, the group can avoid the distraction of empty chatter and sentimentalism by sticking to the sacred text as it is experienced in the lectio and meditatio. The text, the commentary, and the personal response to the text must always be the focus of the discussion. This attention prevents the group from degenerating into frivolous talk about matters unrelated to the text at hand.

Second, debate and dispute within the group erode its focus and purpose. The purpose of collatio is not to get all the answers right. Such behavior causes opposition and division, which destroy the supportive bond of the group. No longer is the group a community of learners, but a collection of individuals with a desire to assert themselves and their own ideas. In a community setting, it is often wise to "agree to disagree."

Third, doctrinaire hairsplitting wears down the spirit of the group. Those who delight in posing subtle questions of details and dogmatic accuracy are unfaithful to the spirit of collatio. An inflexible, pedantic attitude blocks the way to a vital and fulfilling understanding of the passage. With God's word there is no final word, because a final word is a dead word. The Scriptures are the living word of God, the full meaning of which we can never exhaust.

In the group experience of lectio divina, we should strive for conversation in a spirit of love. We should try to share our insights and experiences freely so that we can enlighten and inform one another. As members of the group, we should express ourselves in "I" language in order to make clear that our words come from our own mind and heart.

It is usually helpful to have someone to guide the process of collatio. This guide is usually called a facilitator, as distinguished from a teacher or leader. The facilitator need not be an expert, either in Scripture or in the process of lectio divina. Rather, the facilitator is a person with the simple human skills necessary to guide a group.

The group facilitator for lectio divina performs tasks such as the following:

- assuring members that each one is welcome;
- guiding the group through each phase of the collatio;
- helping keep the group focused on the Scripture;
- ensuring that everyone is able to speak and share insights;
- keeping the group from getting bogged down in dispute;
- helping members believe that their contribution is important to the whole;
- keeping time so that the group keeps moving through each phase and ends on time;
- praying for the welfare of each member of the group.

Keeping in mind this advice and these warnings, we can create a collatio in which thoughts, emotions, opinions, and experiences are peacefully shared and compared. A spirit of mutual support and loving encouragement can create a community truly centered on Christ and illuminated by his word.

Methods of *Collatio*

The group method of lectio divina created by Cardinal Martini, as introduced previously, was quite a remarkable feat. He gathered thousands of youth in the cathedral of Milan and in the churches of his diocese, at their request, to teach them how to pray with Scripture. They gathered on the first Thursday of each month to reflect on the sacred text in prayer and silence.

The session usually began by reciting or chanting a psalm to create the atmosphere of prayerful listening, followed by a few words about the method being used. The lectio began with the reading of the passage from the Bible. The passages were selected thematically—a few months on the prayers of the Bible, then a series on the psalms, then God's call in Scripture, then women of the Bible, etc. The reading of the passage was followed by an explanation of the text and a meditation. This led up to the time for contemplation—fifteen minutes of absolute silence spent in adoration.

Martini insisted that the secret of the success of this work lay in the fact that he did not offer the young people a homily or catechism lesson. Rather, the collatio put them face to face with the scriptural text so they could experience lectio divina for themselves. It taught them to meditate personally on the text and gave them a taste for lectio divina. When they learned to discover their own insights, discern the relationship of the text to their own lives, and feel stimulated to pray, the young people experienced an interior joy. Then, with their taste for lectio divina developed, they continued to discover the richness of Scripture through their own meditation and prayer.

My own work in lectio divina consists of a series of publications called *Threshold Bible Study*.[2] Its method is a combination of contemporary Bible study and the ancient art of lectio divina. The biblical texts used are ordered by themes, with each book of thirty texts organized according to topics, such as the cross, the resurrection, the Holy Spirit, the names of Jesus, the Eucharist, angels, ecology, Advent, the divine heart, Jewish feasts, pilgrimage, and Jerusalem.

Each day individuals read a text followed by a biblical commentary. This lectio leads into a personal meditation through the use of reflection questions. Some questions help participants meditate on a passage of the text and think about it more deeply, others create a dialogue between the text and their life experiences, and still others challenge them to create practical applications for the text in their own lives. Each daily lesson concludes with a prayer based on the biblical text, the commentary, and the meditation. This prayer may be the start of the individual's own personal prayer from the heart.

This daily personal encounter with the word of God may be integrated with a weekly collatio in a small-group format. After reflecting on the daily Scriptures for the week, participants enter the group with the fruit of their own meditation. They discuss their responses to the reflection questions for the purpose of enriching one another. Through shared insights, deeper understanding, and mutual support, the group gradually forms a community of faith, centered on the word of God. Each group session closes with vocal prayer and a few moments of silent contemplation.

There are many effective methods of collatio, but one simple and popular method can be approached using only the Sunday gospel as the text. This format works well with small groups of four to twelve people. After explaining the process step-by-step, the facilitator invites participants to relax in God's presence and calls upon the Holy Spirit.

The first step is a slow and careful reading of the text, allowing each phrase to sink in as the group listens. The reading is followed by a period of silence. Then, one by one, participants repeat a word or phrase that struck them personally.

The second step is another slow reading of the text. This time it may be read by a different reader, perhaps of the opposite sex from the first reader. This will be a deeper listening experience because the word each person shared has enriched the passage for the others. After the second reading, the facilitator invites participants to make applications to their own lives and then share them with the group. They are asked to reflect on the question, "Where does the content of this text touch my life today?" Contributions should be personal, honest, and brief, using "I" language rather than "we" or "you"; for example, "I sense that God wants me to. . . ." There will be lots of thoughtful, prayerful silences. Listeners should use these opportunities to let God's message slowly resonate within them.

The third step is a final reading of the text. After this listening, spontaneous prayers from the group are spoken aloud to God. These prayers should be addressed directly to God, for example, "I ask you, God, for. . . ." or "I am grateful for. . . ."

Close with an extended time of silence, simply resting in the presence of God. A spoken prayer or song may conclude the silence.

Questions for Reflection or Discussion

1. What has been your experience of sharing in a group rooted in God's word? What are the benefits of such a group?

2. In what way is the experience of listening, reflecting, discussing, and praying with Scripture in a group like sharing a meal?

3. What are some tendencies in groups that could erode the spirit of collatio? What are ways to prevent these from multiplying in groups?

4. What are some positive ways to nurture a spirit of mutual support and loving encouragement in a small community centered on the inspired word?

5. What was the reason for the enormous success of the collatio of Cardinal Martini in the diocese of Milan?

6. How might you begin to create small, Scripture-centered communities in your parish or community?

Chapter Nine

The Practice of *Lectio Divina*

We have seen from the long tradition of lectio divina that there are many ways in which we can practice it. As long as we keep in mind the essence of the tradition, we can adapt various methods to our own needs for the prayerful reading of Scripture. The primary aim of lectio divina is the establishment of an intimate dialogue with God through the sacred page. Listening to the voice of God within Scripture, reflecting on the text's personal meaning for us, and responding to God in prayer is the heart of the ancient tradition.

Through expectant faith, we encounter the living Christ through the Scriptures, both the Old and New Testaments. He calls us to be disciples and invites us into an ever-deeper unity with himself. Through the continual practice of lectio divina, we take on the mind and heart of Christ and live more and more in him. Our interior being and our outward expression become more and more conformed to Christ, and we increasingly experience his intimate relationship with the Father and share in that divine unity through the indwelling of the Holy Spirit.

Suggestions for a Personal Method

Lectio. Choose a text of Scripture that you want to read prayerfully. It might be a passage from a biblical book that you are slowly working through, or it might be a passage related to a biblical theme you are focusing on, or it might be the liturgical reading for the day. In a comfortable and quiet place, you might want to light a candle, say a prayer, or offer some other gesture to highlight the moment. Take the Bible in your hands, and turn to your chosen passage. Read the passage slowly and carefully, even aloud if you wish, taking note of any words or phrases that strike you personally. Remember that God is teaching you to listen to his voice within the words of the inspired text.

Meditatio. Spend some time reflecting on the text you have read, personalizing the passage in some way. Allow it to interact with your inner world of memories, ideas, and concerns. Ask yourself what the text means to you and what message it may have for you. If the text is a narrative, use your imagination and enter the scene yourself, envisioning what you experience there and how you respond to the encounter. Repeat and ponder whatever words or phrases strike you from your reading.

Oratio. Speak to God in response to the words, ideas, and images in your reading. Offer to God what you have discovered in yourself from your meditation. Pray to him from your heart in whatever way you wish to reply to the divine word spoken to you. Interact with him as you would with one who knows you intimately, cares about you deeply, and accepts you unconditionally.

Contemplatio. After words cease to be helpful and are no longer necessary, simply rest in God's embrace. In silent stillness, receptively allow him to fill your heart with his divine presence. You do not have to do anything; just place yourself under his loving gaze. Then when he invites you to go back to your inner dialogue with him or to return to meditation on his word, do so. You may freely move to any point on the circle of lectio divina at any time. Often you will return several times to the scriptural text, rereading and searching again for another word or phrase to personalize and ponder. Let God's Spirit guide the entire process of your sacred reading.

Operatio. Sacred reading is a way of letting God's word shape us and change us. Consider the transforming effects of your prayerful reading in your heart and in your daily life. Ask how you are different as a result of this encounter with the word of God: How is your life changing and being shaped through your lectio divina? How does God want you to be different today as a result of this encounter?"

The examples below present an array of biblical texts and a sampling of ideas for the prayerful reading of these texts. The suggested thoughts and questions for reflection are not meant to suggest a rigid method of practice but a variety of adaptable approaches using the primary movements of lectio divina.

Writing and Journaling with *Lectio Divina*

As people practice their lectio, it is helpful for some to write in their Bible or in a journal. If they can convince themselves to take pen or pencil to the sacred page, some are able to enhance their careful reading by marking up the scriptural texts. There is nothing wrong with highlighting and underlining passages, starring verses and circling words, and generally marking up one's Bible. In fact, it seems to me that a well-used Bible is a greater tribute to the word of God than a pristine Bible sitting on a shelf with its gold-leaf pages intact. Marking passages can be a great way of focusing on particular phrases, and it allows for an easy return to particular verses for reflection.

The monks of the early centuries used to compile a *florile-gium*, an anthology of biblical verses that had spoken to them in prayer. They would write a verse or two of their daily lectio in a book, so that eventually this lectio journal preserved a record of their devoted reading. We can follow the same practice today by keeping a journal of the verses through which God's word has spoken most profoundly to us. The act of carefully writing out the text becomes a part of our lectio and meditatio. It represents an act of reverence for the sacred text and becomes a way of assimilating it in order to stay with it longer and remember it more easily.

Those who find writing helpful for prayer may also want to write a response to the scriptural text in their journal. It may take the form of a free-flowing meditation or a prayer addressed to God. This type of writing helps us keep in touch with the experience of lectio divina through the days, weeks, and months of our practice. A written record of prayerful reflection can help us remember past insights and movements of God's Spirit and also lets us see our progress in the art of divine reading.

The Encounter of Moses at the Burning Bush (Exodus 3:1-15)

Lectio

Find a quiet spot for your lectio. Light a candle and set it in front of you as you place your Bible on your lap. Ask the same Holy Spirit who was with Moses in the desert to fill your heart as you read.

Turn to the passage and read slowly and carefully. Vocalize the words of the text so that you not only read with your eyes but hear with your ears.

[1]Moses was keeping the flock of his father-in-law Jethro, the priest of Midian; he led his flock beyond the wilderness, and came to Horeb, the mountain of God. [2]There the angel of the LORD appeared to him in a flame of fire out of a bush; he looked, and the bush was blazing, yet it was not consumed. [3]Then Moses said, "I must turn aside and look at this great sight, and see why the bush is not burned up." [4]When the LORD saw that he had turned aside to see, God called to him out of the bush, "Moses, Moses!" And he said, "Here I am." [5]Then he said, "Come no closer! Remove the sandals from your feet, for the place on which you are standing is holy ground." [6]He said further, "I am the God of your father, the God of Abraham, the God of Isaac, and the God of Jacob." And Moses hid his face, for he was afraid to look at God.

[7]Then the LORD said, "I have observed the misery of my people who are in Egypt; I have heard their cry on account of their taskmasters. Indeed, I know their sufferings, [8]and I have come down to deliver them from the Egyptians, and to bring them up out of that land to a good and broad land, a land flowing with milk and honey, to the country of the Canaanites, the Hittites, the Amorites, the Perizzites, the Hivites, and the Jebusites. [9]The cry of the Israelites has now come to me; I have also seen how the Egyptians

oppress them. [10]So come, I will send you to Pharaoh to bring my people, the Israelites, out of Egypt."

[11]But Moses said to God, "Who am I that I should go to Pharaoh, and bring the Israelites out of Egypt?" [12]He said, "I will be with you; and this shall be the sign for you that it is I who sent you: when you have brought the people out of Egypt, you shall worship God on this mountain."

[13]But Moses said to God, "If I come to the Israelites and say to them, 'The God of your ancestors has sent me to you,' and they ask me, 'What is his name?' what shall I say to them?" [14]God said to Moses, "I AM WHO I AM." He said further, "Thus you shall say to the Israelites, 'I AM has sent me to you.'" [15]God also said to Moses, "Thus you shall say to the Israelites, 'The LORD, the God of your ancestors, the God of Abraham, the God of Isaac, and the God of Jacob, has sent me to you': This is my name forever, and this my title for all generations."

The primal elements of the created world—the desert, the mountain, and fire—became the setting for God's self-revelation. The desert, that place of dryness and silence, formed the solitary sanctuary in which Moses heard God's voice. Here the people of Israel would be brought for a forty-year retreat to be bonded to God. The mountain, mysteriously reaching into the clouds, would be the place where God's people would encounter God and become his own people. The unconsuming flame in the bush would become the fiery threshold joining the divine presence with the material world. On the mountain, God would appear and speak to Moses "out of the fire" and guide his people with a pillar of fire by night through the desert. The flame evokes God's holiness, mystery, and passion.

Meditatio

Use your imagination to enter the scene of the desert, the mountain, and the fire. Imagine that you are Moses in this encounter. What do you see, hear, smell, taste, and feel? What are you thinking, and what emotions are you experiencing?

Do you hear God calling you? Respond, "Here I am." What personal message is God offering to you in this scene? How reluctant are you to respond to his call? What would it take to respond to him with an obedient heart?

Read the passage again slowly. Repeat and ponder whatever words or phrases from your reading strike you.

Oratio

Hear God speaking to you: "Remove the sandals from your feet, for the place on which you are standing is holy ground." Take off your shoes and pray to God with whatever words arise from your heart.

You may choose to begin with these words: "God of my ancestors, of Abraham, Isaac, and Jacob, I am reluctantly drawn to you as I both fear and desire your presence. You have heard the cry of my suffering, and you want to free me from bondage and renew my life. Give me the courage to respond, 'Here I am,' and to listen to your call to me today."

Continue to pray as your heart directs, in whatever way seems to respond to the divine word spoken to you. Pray to the One who knows you intimately, cares about you deeply, and accepts you unconditionally.

Contemplatio

When words are no longer necessary or helpful, imagine you are in the silence and stillness of the desert. Just sit shoeless in the presence of God and place yourself under his loving gaze. Enjoy these holy moments for as long as you wish.

Recall the sacred name of God, "I AM WHO I AM." Repeat God's name to keep your mind focused, and remain mindfully in his holy presence.

Operatio

The flame of the divine presence has purified your mind and softened your heart. Somehow you have changed as a result of your encounter with God. How has God shaped you through your lectio divina? Moses returned to his people and became God's liberating instrument. How is God transforming your life today through his inspired word?

Elijah Meets God on the Mountain (1 Kings 19:4-13)

Lectio

As you close off the distractions of the day and enter a moment of silence, take your Bible and turn to the passage. Kiss the page and ask God to speak to you through the sacred text as he spoke to his prophets of old.

Isolated and fleeing for his life, Elijah is seeking to relinquish his prophetic mission. Discouraged and desiring his own death, the prophet is burned out and does not want to continue. But God prepares him with food and sends him on the journey to the mountain.

⁴[Elijah] went a day's journey into the wilderness, and came and sat down under a solitary broom tree. He asked that he might die: "It is enough; now, O LORD, take away my life, for I am no better than my ancestors." ⁵Then he lay down under the broom tree and fell asleep. Suddenly an angel touched him and said to him, "Get up and eat." ⁶He looked, and there at his head was a cake baked on hot stones, and a jar of water. He ate and drank, and lay down again. ⁷The angel of the LORD came a second time, touched him, and said, "Get up and eat, otherwise the journey will be too much for you." ⁸He got up, and ate and drank; then he went in the strength of that food forty days and forty nights to Horeb the mount of God. ⁹At that place he came to a cave, and spent the night there.

Then the word of the LORD came to him, saying, "What are you doing here, Elijah?" ¹⁰He answered, "I have been very zealous for the LORD, the God of hosts; for the Israelites have forsaken your covenant, thrown down your altars, and killed your prophets with the sword. I alone am left, and they are seeking my life, to take it away."

¹¹He said, "Go out and stand on the mountain before the LORD, for the LORD is about to pass by." Now there was a great wind, so strong that it was splitting mountains and

breaking rocks in pieces before the LORD, but the LORD was not in the wind; and after the wind an earthquake, but the LORD was not in the earthquake; [12]and after the earthquake a fire, but the LORD was not in the fire; and after the fire a sound of sheer silence. [13]When Elijah heard it, he wrapped his face in his mantle and went out and stood at the entrance of the cave.

The usual signs of God's manifestation—storm, earthquake, and fire—do not reveal God to Elijah. It is only in the "sound of sheer silence" that Elijah is drawn from his dark cave to experience new purpose and direction for his life.

Meditatio

Spend some time reflecting on the passage you have read. Remember that God is teaching you to listen to his voice within the words of the inspired text. Allow it to interact with your own experience of discouragement and hope.

Ask yourself what the scene means to you and what personal message it may have for you. When have you been frustrated and ready to give up? When have you felt distant from God and isolated from others? What strength do you need for the journey?

Why did the quiet sound draw Elijah from the cave? When does God speak to you in unexpected ways? In what ways might you be missing the revelation of God today?

Oratio

Respond to God, whom you have heard in the stillness. Offer to him what you have discovered in yourself from your meditation. Speak words that express whatever new hope and purpose you have discovered.

You may choose to begin with words like these: "Lord God, you manifest yourself in storm, earthquake, and fire. Help me to recognize your voice when you speak to me in silence. I am often discouraged in the bustle of life's challenges, and I long for escape. Draw me forth from my darkness and isolation, and give me the courage to turn my face toward you and listen."

Continue to pray from your heart in response to the God who calls you in stillness.

Contemplatio

Place yourself in the "sound of sheer silence." Know that God can communicate with you in the depths of your heart without words and images. Just rest in silent contemplation of the awesome God who manifested his divine presence to Moses and Elijah on the mountain. Do nothing, and know that God will do whatever is necessary to speak to you.

If God invites you to go back to your inner dialogue with him or to return to meditation on the Scripture, do so. Let God's Spirit guide the entire process.

Operatio

God gave Elijah renewed strength and a new mission as a result of his manifestation on the mountain. What have you learned about yourself through your encounter with God's word? What new hope and renewed sense of mission have you received? How will God's word change your life today?

How Long, O Lord?—A Lament (Psalm 13)

Lectio

This psalm of personal lament has been prayed for thousands of years by Israelites and Christians as an expression of anguish in the face of suffering. The haunting question, "How long?" expresses a growing urgency in the face of God's seeming absence. The vague and general language of the lament explains its long-standing popularity, since it can apply to anyone facing an enduring struggle.

Slowly articulate the words of the psalm or chant them plaintively. Hear the words of generations who have sung this lament before you and join in their trusting complaint to God.

¹How long, O Lord? Will you forget me forever?
   How long will you hide your face from me?
²How long must I bear pain in my soul,
   and have sorrow in my heart all day long?
How long shall my enemy be exalted over me?
³Consider and answer me, O Lord my God!
   Give light to my eyes, or I will sleep the sleep of death,
⁴and my enemy will say, "I have prevailed";
   my foes will rejoice because I am shaken.
⁵But I trusted in your steadfast love;
   my heart shall rejoice in your salvation.
⁶I will sing to the Lord,
   because he has dealt bountifully with me.

Most people don't pray this way today. We consider such complaint to be irreverent in the face of a caring and faultless God. But the psalmists prayed out of their concrete situations and poured out their emotions with honest abandon. They did not share our mistaken notion that we must be on our best behavior before God. The ability to express complaint, anger, bitterness, or anguish before God conveys a real and trusting relationship.

The "enemies" in the psalm need not be individuals. They may be forces within society that seem to prevail—such as greed, injustice, bigotry, and hypocrisy—or tendencies within ourselves, such as addictions, prejudice, resentment, and hopelessness. All of these are enemies that seem to prevail over us and leave us in anguish. We plead with God to deliver us from these foes.

The psalmist finally helps us to discover that beneath these painful emotions it is still possible to trust in God. Through praying the lament, the psalmist remembers the fidelity of God and knows that he will hear and answer his prayer. With confidence, the psalm moves from lament to thanksgiving.

Meditatio

Make the prayer of the psalmist become your own prayer. Allow it to interact with your own pain, anguish, failure, humiliation, or resentment. What phrases are most striking for your own situation? Concerning what suffering do you ask of God, "How long"?

Consider the lament of people you know who are suffering. Reflect on those in the hospital, those in prison, those experiencing wars, famines, and natural disasters. Let the psalm become the prayer of suffering humanity.

Oratio

Pray the psalm again from your own heart. Add your own words. Pour out your complaint to God. Acknowledge your anger, bitterness, and loneliness—all of those emotions we so desperately try to suppress because our culture does not approve of them. Forget about being polite and staid before the One who knows you intimately and accepts you unconditionally.

We never pray the psalms in isolation. We join with the prayer of God's people throughout the world who pray these same ancient and inspired prayers. We are not the only ones suffering or feeling abandoned by God. The psalms invite us to move from individual prayer and enter into communion with others. If the words of this lament do not match our own feelings, then we can pray these words with others and for others who are suffering today.

You can pour out your lament to God because you know that honestly expressing your grief before him will lead you to greater trust in his mercy. You can present your suffering and the grief of all God's people before the One who has been faithful in the past, and you can be confident that he will listen to the prayers of the brokenhearted.

Contemplatio

When words are no longer useful or necessary, simply rest in God's embrace. When you cry out to him, know that he attends to your prayers. Trust in his steadfast love and compassion.

The psalms are the prayers of Jesus himself. Through the joys and sufferings of his life, he has voiced these words to the Father. They express what he has felt in the depths of his heart. So you can offer these prayers to God in union with him. Turn to the heart of Jesus, and place your own heart in his.

Operatio

The inspired prayers of Scripture shape and mold our hearts. Praying the prayers of Jesus helps us to conform our hearts to his. How has pouring out your grief to God led you to trust him more? How has praying with and for suffering people made you more compassionate? Resolve today to deepen your trust in God and your compassion for yourself and others around you.

Surrendering to God's All-searching Presence (Psalm 139)

Lectio

Take your Bible from its place of honor and put it in your lap. Become aware of your breathing, slowly inhaling and exhaling, as you put aside the concerns of the day. Turn to Psalm 139 and begin to read out loud slowly as you pray the passage.

As you find phrases in the psalm that touch your heart, pause for meditatio, oratio, or contemplatio. Then return to lectio. You may choose to write out one or two verses that touch you deeply.

> ¹O LORD, you have searched me and known me.
> ²You know when I sit down and when I rise up;
>   you discern my thoughts from far away.
> ³You search out my path and my lying down,
>   and are acquainted with all my ways.

⁴Even before a word is on my tongue,
 O LORD, you know it completely.
⁵You hem me in, behind and before,
 and lay your hand upon me.
⁶Such knowledge is too wonderful for me;
 it is so high that I cannot attain it.

⁷Where can I go from your spirit?
 Or where can I flee from your presence?
⁸If I ascend to heaven, you are there;
 if I make my bed in Sheol, you are there.
⁹If I take the wings of the morning
 and settle at the farthest limits of the sea,
¹⁰even there your hand shall lead me,
 and your right hand shall hold me fast.
¹¹If I say, "Surely the darkness shall cover me,
 and the light around me become night,"
¹²even the darkness is not dark to you;
 the night is as bright as the day,
 for darkness is as light to you.

¹³For it was you who formed my inward parts;
 you knit me together in my mother's womb.
¹⁴I praise you, for I am fearfully and wonderfully made.
 Wonderful are your works;
that I know very well.
 ¹⁵My frame was not hidden from you,
when I was being made in secret,
 intricately woven in the depths of the earth.

[16]Your eyes beheld my unformed substance.
In your book were written
    all the days that were formed for me,
    when none of them as yet existed.
[17]How weighty to me are your thoughts, O God!
    How vast is the sum of them!
[18]I try to count them—they are more than the sand;
    I come to the end—I am still with you.

[19]O that you would kill the wicked, O God,
    and that the bloodthirsty would depart from me—
[20]those who speak of you maliciously,
    and lift themselves up against you for evil!
[21]Do I not hate those who hate you, O LORD?
    And do I not loathe those who rise up against you?
[22]I hate them with perfect hatred;
    I count them my enemies.
[23]Search me, O God, and know my heart;
    test me and know my thoughts.
[24]See if there is any wicked way in me,
    and lead me in the way everlasting.

The four sections of the psalm speak to the intimate relationship between the psalmist and God. God knows the poet completely (verses 1-6), is present wherever the poet is (verses 7-12), and was even present before the poet's birth (verses 13-16).

Even the final section, which reveals the poet's hatred for the wicked (verses 19-22), is a Hebrew way of speaking about the psalmist's intimacy with God and his distance from evildoers.

Although it may seem shocking to us, it is another way of describing the poet's existence as totally within the knowledge, work, and ways of God.

Meditatio

The theme of the whole psalm seems to be the poet's awe-filled exclamation to God, "You know me!" Read the psalm again with a focus on the many ways that God knows you intimately. Pause to reflect each time a phrase speaks to you.

When you reveal private information about yourself to another person, you increase the depth of your bond. Imagine the closeness of your relationship to God, who knew you even before you were born. Consider the feelings that arise within you at the thought of such familiarity with him.

Oratio

Choose the phrases that have most spoken to your heart. Use these words as the foundation for your own heartfelt prayer to God. Express the thoughts and feelings that spring up within you and address them to him. Remember that he knows you intimately and cares about every aspect of your existence.

Contemplatio

The psalmist says that God's intimate knowledge of him is too wonderful to comprehend. Rest in the wonder of his loving care for you. Know that the God who knows you through and through also loves you without measure. Relax in that confidence.

Choose whichever word or phrase you want to ponder. Let that word call you back to the stillness of God's presence. After your prayer of quiet, take that word with you and repeat it occasionally throughout the day.

Operatio

What are the transforming effects of the fact that God knows you so thoroughly? How is your life being shaped and changed by such complete divine knowledge? In what way does his knowledge and love of you lead you to want to know and love others? What can I do today to allow him to "lead me in the way everlasting"?

Jesus and the Little Children (Mark 10:13-16)

Lectio

In your quiet place, turn to the gospel text and ask the Holy Spirit to guide your listening. Read aloud from the text while listening with the ears of your heart.

> [13]People were bringing little children to him in order that he might touch them; and the disciples spoke sternly to them. [14]But when Jesus saw this, he was indignant and said to them, "Let the little children come to me; do not stop them; for it is to such as these that the kingdom of God belongs. [15]Truly I tell you, whoever does not receive the kingdom of God as a little child will never enter it." [16]And he took them up in his arms, laid his hands on them, and blessed them.

Notice that Jesus is described as "indignant" with his disciples for hindering the approach of the children. Jesus welcomed, embraced, and blessed them. Jesus' saying, "For it is to such as these that the kingdom of God belongs," can be interpreted to refer either to these and other children or to people who are like children. Verse 15 highlights those who are like children, and verse 16 underscores the blessedness of the children themselves.

As Jesus took the children in his arms and blessed them, he offered all disciples a lesson about how to be blessed and how to receive God's kingdom. With the trust and confidence of children, we can receive the gifts he wants to give to us.

Kiss the sacred page with reverence and gratitude for God's word to you.

Meditatio

Read the passage again while engaging your full imagination. Imagine you are one of the disciples being reprimanded and taught a lesson by Jesus. What do you notice as the scene unfolds? What is Jesus teaching you? What will you remember most?

Read the passage again, imagining you are one of the children brought to Jesus. What are you seeing, hearing, smelling, and feeling? Experience Jesus welcoming you. See his smile, feel his arms around you, hear his encouraging words, experience his tenderness and his delight in you.

What is different if I come to Jesus as a child, rather than as an adult? What is it like to feel so desired and loved by Jesus? What do I want to remember from this experience?

Oratio

Having heard the words and imagined the touch of Jesus, respond to him in any way you wish. Try to imitate the genuine spontaneity of a child as you speak words of prayer. Express sentiments of delight, joy, trust, reliance, gratitude, confidence, or whatever emotion fills your heart.

Contemplatio

Can you picture yourself just resting in the embrace of Jesus? If this is a comfortable experience for you, just remain there in your imagination for as long as you want. There is no longer any need to respond with words. Just let yourself receive his delight in you. Imagine what it would be like to be totally confident of his love and to trust him completely. Relax.

Operatio

How is God shaping your heart through the divine word? In what ways has this sacred reading renewed and transformed you?

What can you learn from children? How can you be more childlike in your approach to prayer and your relationship to God? What feeling do you want to take with you from this lectio divina today?

The Parable of the Workers in the Vineyard (Matthew 20:1-16)

Lectio

Lectio divina challenges us to encounter each biblical text as if we were reading it for the first time. Nothing is more deadly for this process than approaching a passage with the attitude of knowing what to expect.

To read a parable, we must enter the story from the inside and forget about our humdrum and predictable responses. By their nature, parables are designed to surprise us and give us insights that we have never had before. We often resist their full impact because they disturb our comfortable way of thinking and revolutionize our understanding of God.

Ask God's Spirit to accompany your reading, and listen to this passage as if for the first time.

[1]"For the kingdom of heaven is like a landowner who went out early in the morning to hire laborers for his vineyard. [2]After agreeing with the laborers for the usual daily wage, he sent them into his vineyard. [3]When he went out about nine o'clock, he saw others standing idle in the marketplace; [4]and he said to them, 'You also go into the vineyard, and I will pay you whatever is right.' So they went. [5]When he went out again about noon and about three o'clock, he did the same. [6]And about five o'clock he went out and found others standing around; and he said to them, 'Why are you standing here idle all day?' [7]They said to him, 'Because no one has hired us.' He said to them, 'You also go into the vineyard.' [8]When evening came, the owner of the vineyard said to his manager, 'Call the laborers and give them their pay, beginning with the last and then going to the first.' [9]When those hired about five o'clock came, each of them received the usual daily wage. [10]Now when the first came, they thought they would receive more; but each of them also received the usual daily wage. [11]And when they received it, they grumbled against the landowner, [12]saying, 'These last

worked only one hour, and you have made them equal to us who have borne the burden of the day and the scorching heat.' [13]But he replied to one of them, 'Friend, I am doing you no wrong; did you not agree with me for the usual daily wage? [14]Take what belongs to you and go; I choose to give to this last the same as I give to you. [15]Am I not allowed to do what I choose with what belongs to me? Or are you envious because I am generous?' [16]So the last will be first, and the first will be last."

A story like this one, in which the vineyard owner paid all his laborers the same wage no matter how long they had worked, is not one that many people would dare allow themselves to take to heart. But the impact of the parable on the disciples of Jesus and on early Christian readers was powerful for those who allowed themselves to fully enter it. The vineyard owner claimed the right to pay his workers not on the basis of their merit but on the basis of his own compassion. Does this mean that God is unfair or exceptionally generous? As you reflect on what this story is really saying, remember that Jesus' parables are intended to turn our thoughts upside down.

Meditatio

Jesus said that in reaction to his parables the hearts of many would grow hard. Why? Because many people will not dare allow themselves to hear a parable with a listening heart and open themselves to its implications for their lives. What is this parable doing to your heart?

How do the grumbling workers of verse 12 express your resentment of the parable? How does the parable challenge your sense of justice? Why is the parable so offensive to you? How does the last question of Jesus startle you, "Are you envious because I am generous?"

If you are a latecomer to faith in God, how does this parable make you feel? Can you possibly accept the extravagant generosity and mercy of God? How does this parable challenge your usual ways of thinking about God?

Oratio

Speak to God in response to the parable. Pray with honesty, forsaking the need to be polite and reserved in his presence. Tell him whatever comes to mind as you hear the words of Jesus. Articulate your feelings to the One who accepts you completely.

You may want to pray in this way: "Lord Jesus, your words are startling and disturb my comfortable ways of thinking about God. I am confused by a God who doesn't meet my standards of fairness. Help me receive your parable with an open heart, and let it penetrate my spirit. Let it turn my picture of God upside down and challenge me to overturn my expectations. If you are to be my Lord, you will not let me be a conventional Christian. Give me your Spirit so that I may be challenged to radical discipleship." Continue with your own prayer.

Contemplatio

Accept the presence of the One who overturns the status quo of your life. Realize that God is transforming you and molding you from the inside, even if you are not aware of it.

Remain in quiet and stillness, allowing the unfathomable God to be your God.

Operatio

Consider the practical challenges presented to you by the parable. Could you possibly give others the love they need, rather than the love they earn? What impact would such a radical way of living make on your life today?

The Storm on the Sea (Mark 4:35-41)

Lectio

When you have settled into a quiet place, open your Bible to the passage. Ask God to speak to you and help you hear his voice in the gospel. Read the text aloud, pausing to reflect on the words. Be attentive to the details.

[35]On that day, when evening had come, [Jesus] said to them, "Let us go across to the other side." [36]And leaving the crowd behind, they took him with them in the boat, just as he was. Other boats were with him. [37]A great windstorm arose, and the waves beat into the boat, so that the boat was already being swamped. [38]But he was in the stern, asleep on the cushion; and they woke him up and said to him, "Teacher, do you not care that we are perishing?" [39]He woke up and rebuked the wind, and said to the sea, "Peace! Be still!" Then the wind ceased, and there was a dead calm. [40]He said to them, "Why are you afraid? Have you still no faith?" [41]And they were filled with great awe and said to

one another, "Who then is this, that even the wind and the sea obey him?"

After a full day of teaching from the boat, Jesus was tired and desired to go to the other side of the Sea of Galilee, away from the crowd. Knowing the dangers of sudden storms on the lake, the disciples feared for their lives when the boat began to be swamped by the waves. Jesus' command to the wind and waves was simple and brief, yet these natural forces obeyed him.

This gospel scene offered great consolation to the early church in the midst of terrible turmoil and persecution. It appealed to its early readers to trust Jesus, who is Lord of his church. They could rely on him to control the chaotic forces of nature and history, just as the God of Israel had brought order out of chaos and directed his people not to fear.

Meditatio

After reflecting on how this parable impacted its first readers, we are challenged to actualize it, to bring God's word into the present. By reflecting on its relevance to our own circumstances, we can offer a sincere response to the scriptural text.

How does Jesus' calming of the sea affect you today? What aspects of your concrete situation does the text highlight? How does the text speak God's word to your life?

Reflect on the fears and "storms" in your life right now. Imagine Jesus in the midst of your turmoil. Let Jesus speak these words to you: "Why are you afraid? Have you still no faith?" Ponder his words and let them penetrate you. How do they resonate within you?

Oratio

Your prayer might go something like this: "God, I have so many fears (name your fears). Perhaps my biggest fear is that you are asleep, that you are not paying attention to my anxieties, that you don't care if I perish in the storm. Help me to trust in you, to believe that you are present in the tempest, and that you have power over the wind and the waves. Calm my fears and let me believe that you are the Lord of my life."

Respond to God in the midst of whatever storm you are facing. Believe that he can bring you from fear to trust. Tell him of your cares and worries, your confidence and trust, your faith and hope.

Contemplatio

As you run out of words, just imagine yourself in the boat with Jesus. "Peace! Be still!" he says. Rest with confidence in his presence, and entrust your worries to him. Spend some quiet moments in peace with Christ. Whenever worries and distractions arise in your mind, repeat the words of Jesus, "Peace. Be still!"

Operatio

Consider the source of your fears. Try letting go of one worry at a time. Consider how your prayerful reading of this text is leading you to deeper trust.

Choose a word or short phrase from the text to take with you. Repeat that word or phrase throughout your day, and have confidence that your life is slowly being shaped through God's word in your midst.

Continuing to Pray with Scripture

As the book of Christ's church, the Bible is a God-given way to experience the divine presence. Its inspired words not only offer us a treasury of images, stories, portraits of faith, prayers, and prophetic challenges, but they also bring us into an encounter with the living God. They are his words, personally addressed to us, and they have the power to convert our hearts and transform our lives.

Hopefully, after reading *Conversing with God in Scripture*, you are more aware of this truth. As an introduction to the long and rich tradition of lectio divina, this book is only meant to be a beginning for you. It invites you into a lifelong experience of reading the sacred text as the threshold to a more personal relationship with Christ. It is my hope that you will commit to make prayerful reading of the Bible the heart of your Christian life. As you make even the smallest effort to seek the Lord, realize that he awaits you with open arms. "Listen! I am standing at the door, knocking; if you hear my voice and open the door, I will come in to you and eat with you, and you with me" (Revelation 3:20).

Questions for Reflection or Discussion

1. What do you consider the most essential aspects of lectio divina?

2. What are the advantages of keeping a lectio journal? How would you like to integrate writing into your practice of lectio divina?

3. The texts centered on the encounters of Moses and Elijah with God are examples of the literary form called a "theophany"— a description of a personal encounter with God. Describe your experience of practicing lectio divina with a theophany.

4. What was unique or different for you in practicing lectio divina with the psalms?

5. Compare your experience of prayerfully reading the three gospel passages. What elements do you want to integrate into your own personal practice of lectio divina?

6. What did you find to be most encouraging and motivating in this study of lectio divina?

Notes

Chapter 1:
Return to *Lectio Divina*: A New Moment for the Church

1. Jerome, *Commentaries on Isaiah,* 18, Prologue: *Patrologia Latina* 24, 17b.

2. Jerome, *Commentaries on the Letter to Titus,* 3, 9.

3. Louis Bouyer, *The Word, Church and Sacrament: In Protestantism and Catholicism* (San Francisco: Ignatius Press, 2004), p. 16.

4. Pope Benedict XVI, addressing participants of the International Congress on the fortieth Anniversary of Dei Verbum, Rome, September 16, 2005, *Dei Verbum Bulletin,* N. 76/77 (2005), p. 5.

5. *Dei Verbum Bulletin,* N. 76/77 (2005), p. 5.

6. Jerome, *Letters,* 3, 4: *Patrologia Latina* 22, 134.

7. Gregory, *Letters,* 31, 54: *Patrologia Latina* 77, 706.

8. Augustine, *Sermons,* 63: *Patrologia Latina* 38, 424.

9. Quoted by Eltin Griffin, "Lectio Divina," http://carmelites.ie /Spirituality/lectiodivina.html.

Chapter 2:
A Living Book, Centered in Christ

1. Quoted by Eltin Griffin, O.Carm., "Lectio Divina."

2. Jerome, *Commentaries on the Letter to the Galatians* 5, 19-21: *Patrologia Latina* 26, 417a.

3. Origen, *Homilies on Genesis,* hom. 9-1: *Patrologia Graeca* 12, 210.

4. Augustine, *Quaestiones in heptateuchum* 2, 73: *Patrologia Latina* 34, 623.

5. Hugh of St. Victor, *The Ark of Noah,* 2, 8: *Patrologia Latina* 176, 642c.

6. Augustine, *Tractates on the Gospel of John*, 24, 7: *Patrologia Latina* 35, 1596.

7. Augustine, *Explanations of the Psalms*, 103, 4, 1: *Patrologia Latina* 37, 1378.

8. Adapted from *The Ascent of Mt. Carmel, 22, 3.* in *The Works of St. John of the Cross* (London: Hasell, Watson, & Viney, Ltd., 1922), http://www.google.com/books.

9. Jerome, *Letters,* 22, 25: *Patrologia Latina,* 22, 411.

10. Bernard of Clairvaux, *Sermons on the Canticle of Canticles,* serm. 23, n. 3: *Patrologia Latina* 183, 885d.

11. Jerome, *Commentary on Ecclesiastes,* 3: *Patrologia Latina* 23, 1039a.

Chapter 3:

Lectio: Reading the Text with a Listening Ear

1. *Scala Claustralium, Sources Chretiennes* 163 (Paris: Cerf, 1942); *The Ladder of Monks and Twelve Meditations by Guigo II* (Garden City, NY: Doubleday Image Books, 1978).

2. *Scala Claustralium* 2, *Sources Chretiennes* 163, pp. 82–84.

3. *Scala Claustralium* 2, *Sources Chretiennes* 163, pp. 82–84.

4. *Scala Claustralium* 12, *Sources Chretiennes* 163, p. 108.

5. Thomas Keating, *"The Classical Monastic Practice of Lectio Divina,"* http://www.centeringprayer.com/lectio/lectio.htm.

6. M. Basil Pennington, *Lectio Divina: Renewing the Ancient Practice of Praying the Scriptures* (New York: Crossroad, 1998), pp. 88–89.

7. Pennington, pp. 70–78.

8. Thelma Hall, *Too Deep For Words: Rediscovering Lectio Divina* (New York: Paulist Press, 1988), p. 28.

9. Benedict, *The Rule of Saint Benedict*, Prologue.

10. Ambrose, *Orationes sive meditations*, Prologue.

11. Pontifical Biblical Commission, *The Interpretation of the Bible in the Church* (Vatican City, 1993), III, C, 1.

Chapter 4:

Meditatio: Reflecting on the Meaning and
Message of the Text

1. Ambrose, *Commentaries on the Psalms* I, 33: *Patrologia Latina* 14, 984.

2. *Scala Claustralium* 2, *Sources Chretiennes* 163, pp. 82-84.

3. *Lettera gesta docet, quid credas allegoria, moralis quid agas, quo tendas anagogia.*

Chapter 5:

Oratio: Praying in Response to God's Word

1. Thelma Hall, *Too Deep For Words: Rediscovering Lectio Divina* (New York: Paulist Press, 1988), p. 44.

2. Augustine, *The Confessions of St. Augustine*, Book 1, Chap. 1, #2, tr. John K. Ryan (New York: Doubleday Image Books, 1960), p. 43.

3. Augustine, *Explanations of the Psalms*, 37,14: *Patrologia Latina* 36, 404.

Chapter 6:

Contemplatio: Quietly Resting in God

1. Thomas Keating, *"The Classical Monastic Practice of Lectio Divina,"* http://www.centeringprayer.com/lectio/lectio.htm.

Chapter 7:

Operatio: Faithful Witness in Daily Life

1. Hugh of St. Victor, *The Ark of Noah*, 2, 8: *Patrologia Latina* 176, 642c.

2. Carlo M. Martini, "Lectio Divina," *Dei Verbum Bulletin*, N. 10, (1989), pp. 16–18.

3. *The Interpretation of the Bible in the Church*, IV, A.2.

Chapter 8:

Collatio: Forming Community Through Scripture

1. Isidore of Seville, *Three Books of Sentences*, 3, 14: *De collatione*: *Patrologia Latina* 83, 688–89.

2. Stephen J. Binz, *Threshold Bible Study*, http://www.threshold biblestudy.com.